FROM THE MOUTHS OF DOGS

FROM *the*

MOUTHS
of DOGS

WHAT OUR PETS TEACH US ABOUT
LIFE, DEATH, AND BEING HUMAN

B.J. Hollars

UNIVERSITY OF NEBRASKA PRESS · LINCOLN AND LONDON

Library of Congress
Cataloging-in-Publication Data
Hollars, B.J.
From the mouths of dogs: what
our pets teach us about life, death,
and being human / B.J. Hollars.
pages   cm
Includes bibliographical references.
ISBN 978-0-8032-7729-8 (cloth: alk. paper)
ISBN 978-0-8032-8491-3 (epub)
ISBN 978-0-8032-8492-0 (mobi)
ISBN 978-0-8032-8493-7 (pdf)
1. Dogs—Wisconsin.
2. Dog owners—Wisconsin.
3. Human-animal relationships—
Wisconsin. I. Title.
SF426.H626 2015
636.709775—dc23
2015013300

Set in Garamond Premier
by L. Auten.
Designed by N. Putens.

All his life he tried to be a good person.
Many times, however, he failed. For after
all, he was only human. He wasn't a dog.

—CHARLES M. SCHULTZ

CONTENTS

PART 2. LESSONS LIVED

ACKNOWLEDGMENTS

This book was written with the support of several individuals, all of whom deserve mention.

First and foremost, thank you to the people who were kind enough to share their stories with me, including Patrice Anderson, Scott and Sally Dawson, Rob Gierka, Amber Gooden, Tammy and Ken Gurklis, Bob and Elsbeth Johnson, Terry Kufner, Rexann Lemke, Ed Martin Jr., Margaret McDougall, Kathy Merrell, Kathy Mitchell, Pastor Eric Nielson, Christena O'Brien, Traiden Oleson, Amy Quella, Nikki Ristau, Gail Schellinger, Dr. Katherine Schneider, Sara Stary, Matt Thompson, Mary Thurston, Emily Townsend, Erin Weiss, and Bekah Weitz.

In addition, a special thanks to the Eau Claire County Humane Association, Bob's House for Dogs, the City of Eau Claire, and all other institutions dedicated to animal welfare.

Thank you to my colleagues at the University of Wisconsin–Eau Claire, and in particular, Chancellor James Schmidt, Provost Patricia Kleine, President Kimera Way, Dean David Leaman, Dean Carmen Manning, Dr. Erica Benson, Dr. Audrey Fessler, Dr. Stephanie Turner, Max Garland, Jon Loomis, Allyson Loomis, Molly Patterson, Dr. Justin Patchin, Dr. Jason Spraitz, Joanne Erickson, and Vickie Schafer. I could go on.

Thanks also to my fine assistants, Alex Long, Josh Bauer, and Erin Stevens, all of whom made this book better.

In addition, thank you to Dr. Karen Havholm and the Office of Research and Sponsored Programs at the University of Wisconsin–Eau Claire, whose University Research and Creative Activity grant proved vital to this project.

Thank you to my family who joined me on the epic road trip that became the focus of the book's final chapter. We endured! (And next year we will go to the beach, I promise.)

And finally, a fond farewell to friends' pets who have recently passed, including Ali, Audrey, Bear, Brady, Bryce, Django, Dorie, George, Hugo, Kitty, Leto, Mr. Boo, Nellie, Nina, Penelope, Sagan, Sedgewick, Smoke, Tigger, and so many more. Thanks for enriching our lives.

AUTHOR'S NOTE

What you are about to read is a nonfiction account involving real people and real pets in and around Wisconsin's Chippewa Valley. At their request, I have changed the names of three of my subjects: Scott and Sally Dawson, as well as Emily Townsend, are pseudonyms.

All material within quotation marks is a direct quotation from an interview, newspaper, book, or other source, all of which can be found in the sources section of this book. On rare occasion I employed italics to re-create small portions of historical dialogue or inner monologue, such as in chapter 5, where I reenvision a conversation between Samuel Johnson and the first woman in need of his future pet cemetery, and in chapter 8, where I try to get inside the head of a pet owner.

The author and his childhood dog, Sandy, circa 1988.
Courtesy of the author.

PROLOGUE

Going to the Dogs

The dog is dead, and we are left to deal with the body. It's not even our dog, but our neighbors', a brindle-colored Plott hound named Dorsey who lived just a few houses down. It's January 2007, and though I have just returned to college to finish my senior year, the distance does little to insulate me from the grief. I am 350 miles away, but I wasn't always and, in fact, had spent quite a bit of time with Dorsey over holiday break because of my parents' dog-watching duties. Throughout Christmas and New Year's, I'd watched his body shrink and unravel, watched that dog become a shadow before my eyes. Some nights my parents, brother, and I took turns holding vigil, curling up along-side Dorsey in our darkened living room, blanketed in the glow of Christmas lights.

Though everyone up and down North Washington Road knew Dorsey, our family knew him better than most. In fact, given his arranged "marriage" to our own dog—a German shepherd mix named Sydney—we were, technically speaking, in-laws. And so, when he finally passed—when Dorsey was found deflated in my parents' bedroom—Sydney became (again, technically speaking) his widow. Having held up her end of the "till death do you part" portion of the vows, Sydney was once again a free dog. But in truth, she'd always been free, and though my overzealous, animal-loving mother had tried to make an honest couple of them, on their so-called wedding day, neither bride nor groom knew matrimony from Marmaduke.

We'd been dog sitting Dorsey that particular weekend as well, which gave my mother ample time to prepare for their nuptials. Thankfully, the preparations didn't go so far as to include flower arrangements and a three-tiered cake, though she did manage to wrap Sydney inside the same wedding dress in which she herself had been married. To give Dorsey his own dose of humiliation, she fit a suit coat around his slumping shoulders and planted a top hat atop his head.

"There," she said, "perfect."

But not quite.

What good was the wedding, after all, if there were no pictures to preserve it?

"Here," she said, handing me the camera, "make sure you get a few close-ups."

Though I much preferred my part as the incredulous, eyebrow-raised gawker, I soon found myself thrust into the role of official wedding photographer, my mother invoking her "I gave you life" argument, which didn't leave me much in the way of rebuttal. Against my better judgment, for an entire roll of film I captured close-ups of those droopy-eared dogs staring forlornly at the camera. It was a memorable day for the humans in the room, though for the newly-weds, one they'd just as soon forget.

∵

In the days leading up to Dorsey's death, I could hardly recognize the skeletal dog stretched before me. Where was the gallant, barrel-chested nighttime howler who for years had wooed our mutt? The passionate nose nuzzler? The dandy of a dog dressed in his top hat and suit? Throughout holiday break, each bone newly poked through his brindled coat reduced him to an anatomy lesson. But the most important lesson he taught us had little to do with his body, but rather involved what we were destined to do with it.

Dorsey died just days after I returned to college. I received the phone call from my mother, who reported to me how Dorsey's human had immediately returned home to retrieve his newly departed dog.

Heartbroken, he'd immediately taken up his shovel, busting through the frozen earth in an attempt to bury the body. He'd succeeded, mostly, but it wasn't until the following spring that a troupe of loyal neighbors and dogs—myself included—gathered in a shady corner of Dorsey's lawn to offer our true good-byes. Alongside Dorsey's previously dug grave we dug a second hole, into which we planted a fern.

I was twenty-two at the time and, thanks to my mother, up until that moment had attended at least one more dog wedding than funeral. However, upon attending my first dog funeral ("memorial service," if we're going to continue speaking technically) I surprised myself by finding the occasion far more sacred than profane. This funeral was no living room wedding shared between reluctant dogs, but a carefully planned ceremony meant to ease our pain.

Though it didn't, at least not right away.

Sure, the hole in the ground was now filled, but not the hole in our hearts. My own grief felt unexpected, unfounded even, particularly because Dorsey wasn't even my dog.

He has his own loving family to grieve for him, I reminded myself as I peered down at his fern, *so why do you feel this way?*

Perhaps because Dorsey had shared something quite intimate with me in his final days, as had my parents, whom I'd watched hand-feed him hot dogs atop my old sleeping bag before carrying him to the bathroom in the backyard snow. Throughout our dog-sitting duties, my family had watched Dorsey grow weak and incontinent and, as the days passed, become more of a shell of a dog than a dog. Thus I reasoned that the grief I felt for him was the result of what he'd given me: a front-row seat to a show I wasn't certain I wanted to see.

That spring, when we gathered to memorialize him, even the dogs in attendance took their best crack at solemnity—participating in a poorly executed four-legged funeral procession. There was no need for pallbearers (not even "pawbearers," as somebody joked) as the hard work of digging Dorsey's grave had been done on a cold winter's night several months prior.

As the ceremony came to its close, I blamed my damp eyes on

allergies, my trembling hands on too much caffeine. We all made our way out of the shade and into the dappled sunlight, at which point we wiped the stray tears from our eyes and continued swapping stories about that dog. As I watched the others begin saying their good-byes and scattering throughout the neighborhood, it occurred to me that aside from the flea scratching and urinating, Dorsey's memorial service had resembled an experience we humans know all too well. Though none of us had ever attended a dog's memorial service before, we all seemed to understand the protocol. We simply did what we'd always done when a loved one died—gathered together, bowed our heads, and waited for life to move on.

∴

The people of North Washington Road were hardly the first to take part in a formal send-off for a beloved animal; the Phoenicians beat us to it by a few thousand years. Between 1985 and 1992, archeologists in Ashkelon, Israel, unearthed the remains of over twelve hundred dogs, earning the burial ground the title of "largest dog cemetery in the ancient world" according to Harvard professor and excavation director Lawrence E. Stager. As Stager explains, for a brief period, the Phoenicians forewent their "profit-making enterprises" in the import-export business in order to more appropriately honor their departed dogs by granting them burial plots along the Mediterranean coast.

Fifteen hundred years later and eight thousand miles away, the pre-Incan Chiribaya people were busy burying dogs themselves. While the view from the ancient cemetery in a Peruvian port city rivaled Ashkelon's own splendor, the amenities for the Chiribayas' dogs remained second to none. Peruvian anthropologist Sonia Guillén discovered the burial plots in the summer of 2006, when she and her team exhumed over eighty canine mummies buried in individual graves alongside their humans. More interesting than the fact that the Chiribayas, like the Phoenicians, buried their dogs, is *how* they chose to bury them. Guillén's team discovered that, prior to burial, many of the dogs were wrapped in llama-wool blankets—the same wrappings, writer Roger Atwood notes, that accompanied "low-ranking people buried nearby." Atwood goes on to report that "llama bones and fish skeletons were placed next to their snouts, showing their owners left treats for them to enjoy in the afterlife." It wasn't exactly the Four Seasons, but the extra bedding and burial-side room service was more than many Chiribaya people could hope for.

Ancient Egyptian culture employed a similar practice of providing "grave goods" to the departed. From pharaohs to laypeople, Egyptians were regularly buried with both practical and extravagant objects—from pottery to golden jewels. These items were believed to assist the deceased in their journey to the afterlife, leading anthropologists to wonder if the llama bones and fish skeletons buried alongside the Chiribaya dogs served a similar purpose—something for them to gnaw on during their postlife travels.

Guillén speculates that the Chiribayas' red-carpeted farewell to their dogs was simply a show of gratitude for their service. "The Chiribaya people raised large numbers of llamas and alpacas," Guillén explains, "and these dogs were considered partners in this work."

While the role of the Chiribaya dogs appears clearly defined, back in Ashkelon, the Phoenicians' dogs performed a more nebulous task. According to Stager, dogs may have earned their seaside plots not due to any specific dog-related duties but due to the role canines played in the Phoenicians' spiritual lives. Stager argues that the dogs may have served as a "healing cult"; that is, a nonmedical answer to a human's mental or physical ailments.

"If anyone has a better explanation for the immense dog cemetery at Ashkelon," Stager writes, "I would like to hear it."

As an alternative, St. Louis University biblical studies professor Geoffrey David Miller set forth his Occam's razor approach to the burials. "The most likely explanation is that the Phoenicians buried dogs to which they had some emotional attachment," Miller reports. "As with most people in the ancient Near East, the Phoenicians valued canines for their role as hunting dogs, sheepdogs, guard dogs and possibly pets."

Dorsey was no hunting dog, no sheepdog, not even much of a guard dog. Nor was he — at least to my knowledge — endowed with the power to cure our mental or physical ailments. His primary function had always been to serve as a loyal pet, which seemed reason enough to provide him a proper burial. Simply put, we buried him because that's how we'd always treated the people — correction, the *pets* — that we loved.

Yet we needn't rely solely on Dorsey's story — or for that matter, the burial practices of pre-Incan empires or ancient Israel — for proof of our love for our pets. In fact, we need look no further than a 2012 study from the American Pet Products Association (APPA), which reports that the United States is home to over 377 million of them. All our creatures — be they finned, feathered, or furred — are spread among nearly 73 million homes, which means, on average, each of these households is home to around five pets. That's not so unbelievable if we're talking goldfish, but the numbers take on an entirely new significance once we subtract fins from the equation. While nearly 160 million of our pets are, in fact, finned (consider the lifespan of a goldfish and you'll understand why), another 78 million are dogs, dogs that we will one day choose to bury or not. But if we do choose to bury them, our decision will likely have little to do with their llama-herding skills or their service to any modern-day healing cults. Instead, we will bury our dogs because we've come to view them as four-legged versions of ourselves, because every tail wag and clear-throated bark serves as further confirmation that they are creatures in possession of emotions, preferences, and, dare I say it, a soul. But mostly we will bury them because we like them, and because they've led us to believe that they like us as well. This is, perhaps, the dog's greatest evolutionary development: an ability to solidify themselves in our good graces by peering soulfully into our eyes.

Of course, pet burial hardly stops with dogs but expands to include a variety of other animals: cats, birds, hamsters, gerbils, even goldfish lucky enough to be spared their usual swirling "burial at sea." For many, the connection a pet owner feels with any of these animals warrants burial; to do otherwise would seem like sacrilege. The heart loves what the heart loves, after all, and sometimes what it happens to love is a lizard.

But perhaps the most practical proof of our love for our pets is found in another statistic provided by the APPA. According to the association, in 2014 U.S. citizens will spend an estimated $58.51 billion on pet expenditures. To put it into perspective, that's over $3 billion more than what's been earmarked for the Department of Homeland Security in the 2013 federal budget. Likewise, NASA — hard at work on their Asteroid Redirect Initiative to defend the planet against life-snuffing asteroids — received a mere $17.8 billion, less than a third of what we are expected to spend on our pets. Thus our priorities become clear: we are far more concerned with Princess's painted toenails than whether or not all life is blown to smithereens.

Now before you go getting your leashes in a knot, take comfort in knowing that most of these animal-related expenses aren't racked up by way of painted toenails, puppy papooses, or cat-sized cowboy boots. Instead, these expenses are mostly earmarked for the essentials — food, vet bills, and kenneling. Though in recent years, the postlife pet industry has continued to make inroads as well. While a hole in the backyard suffices for many pet owners, there is another breed of pet owner who sees fit to honor animals in a more extravagant fashion. Such as Mrs. M. F. Walsh, who in 1915 paid $25,000 to erect a granite mausoleum for her five pets in the heart of Hartsdale Pet Cemetery — the country's largest and oldest pet cemetery — located just outside of Manhattan.

Perhaps it was the pet-loving Mrs. Walsh and people like her who initially led me down this path of trying to better understand our relationships with our pets. While these relationships vary due to any number of cultural considerations, one fact we know for certain is that over the past two centuries, Americans' views on pets have dramatically shifted. This evolution of thought is most often attributed to the rise of urbanization, which placed pet and pet owner in closer proximity than ever before, thereby strengthening the bonds between us.

While there is no shortage of books, theses, and documentaries dedicated to the subject of the human-animal bond, rare is the work that extends beyond this, focusing instead on what we humans stand to learn as a result of our close-knit lives with our pets.

What can a dog teach me, the cynic might ask, *but how to fetch a tennis ball?*

I'd argue that dogs stand to teach us quite a bit more, as do cats and all other domesticated pets. The unspoken lessons we learn from our pets are most valuable for what they reveal about our relationships with them. To this end, while this book may masquerade as a narrative on the human-animal bond, make no mistake, my primary interest remains with the humans. What can pets teach us? Or, to put it differently: what can we learn when we listen?

Keep in mind that I write this not as a scientist, sociologist, or animal behaviorist, but as a humble writer and avid dog walker who, for many laps around the neighborhood, has wondered what lessons might be gleaned from the brazenly disobedient thirteen-pound mixed breed tugging at the end of her leash. Cici has taught me various lessons throughout her life, including the Zen-like qualities of chasing squirrels, chasing cars, and barking at whichever of the two first crosses her field of vision. Though I admit that on occasion I've treaded into the unthinkable realm of wondering what more serious lessons she—much like Dorsey—might teach me in her final days. Including the hardest lesson of all: whether my love for her will one day demand I place her aching body in the passenger seat as we take our final, fated drive to the vet.

I'll admit that my interest in pets, and specifically, what their abbreviated lives might teach us, is directly linked to my own current existential crisis. As I enter my thirties, I've at last reached the point in my life where the luster of youth's immortality has been swiftly replaced by the less-popular mortality. Today I am the proudish owner of a minivan and a mortgage, which is to say: today I feel like my dad.

Yet of far greater concern than my own future farewell is the fear of saying farewell to my loved ones. As a new father, I now think of death differently—no longer an "if" but a "when." My son had hardly left the delivery room before Death transformed from a scythe-wielding cloak to a clock, one whose every tick reminded me that none of us are getting out of here alive. These days, every scraped and skinned knee my son acquires serves as further confirmation that we cannot protect even the people we love the most. Worst still is the notion that when it comes to our pets, not only are we incapable of preventing this pain, but on occasion, we may be the cause of it. And one day, after sharing a life together for so many years, we may be forced to don the cloak and wield the scythe ourselves.

Come on, old girl, get in the car, we'll say. And tragically, that old girl will obey.

It is a pain most can't fathom, but what choice do we have? A life with no pets at all?

If pets have taught me anything, it's that we should never shy away from joy for fear of losing that joy.

A few months back, this lesson hit close to home. My son and I were at the vet awaiting Cici's yearly checkup when I glanced up from the rainbowed rows of dog food to spot a man leaving an exam room unaccompanied by his pet.

My stomach dropped. And it dropped further once I realized that the man was a friend of mine and that I'd inadvertently intruded on his moment of crisis. For weeks, he and I had chatted casually about this very book, about our shared love for our dogs and our fear of letting go. And suddenly there I was witnessing his supremely personal moment, the interloper to his grief.

Upon seeing me he offered a halfhearted smile, then gave Cici a scratch behind the ears.

I bumbled through my long-winded condolences, trying hard to find a string of words that didn't feel canned, words that might offer true comfort.

After I finally made the smart decision to resort to silence instead, my friend opened his mouth to speak.

"You know," he said, his voice wavering, "life might be easier without a dog, but it definitely wouldn't be better."

∵

A year after Dorsey died, my family, too, came to understand heartache. In 2008, upon my parents' decision to euthanize our own ailing dog, Sydney trotted after Dorsey into the Great Beyond. My parents buried Sydney, wrapped in her favorite blanket, in our backyard pet cemetery, just half a mile from her spouse. My father did the digging, as he had for all our past pets—a skill with which he gained such proficiency that within a year of Sydney's death, he'd make a profession of it, digging human graves at a local cemetery. But on the evening following Sydney's death, his task was personal, and with each pound of his boot to the shovel head, his eyes darted to the blanketed body resting in the leaves alongside him.

I regret to admit that there was no funeral for Sydney, no memorial service, not even so much as a planted fern. I was in graduate school in Alabama at the time, while my brother Brian was an undergraduate half the state away. With no children left in the house, perhaps my parents didn't feel the need to organize a formal farewell. As society dictated, they handled their grief privately. My father simply lowered Sydney into the hole, covered her body with dirt, and appropriated a piece of broken brick as a marker. She became just another pet laid to rest in our backyard pet cemetery, joining all the others we'd loved before her.

Meanwhile, six hundred miles away, I sat helpless in my Alabama home. Even after experiencing Dorsey's passing, I still didn't know how to grieve at such a great distance. And so I tried another tack. I told myself that Sydney had exited my life years ago anyway, that since leaving for college, I had known her only as a result of my rare visits home. I told myself that I'd forgotten all about the spring in her step, the bark in her belly, the games she used to play. I told myself she was just some stinky, old, snaggle-toothed dog, nothing more.

Just some dog, I thought as the tears streamed down, *to whom I'd given my heart*.

PART 1

.....

Lessons Learned

ONE

·····

SNIFFING FOR TROUBLE

The greatness of a nation and its moral progress can

be judged by the way its animals are treated.

—MAHATMA GANDHI

One early Saturday morning in the fall of 2009, I received a phone call from a neighbor friend in need of assistance. She'd been biking Alabama's rural roads when she stumbled upon a puppy hobbling in the tall grass.

"You found a puppy?" I asked. "What kind?"

"The tiny kind."

Laying her bike to the edge of the road, she kept that puppy company until my blue Ford Focus pulled alongside them half an hour later.

After I stepped from the car and examined the puppy, it became clear she wasn't joking about its size. The puppy *was* tiny—tinier than tiny—and more closely resembled a poorly fed pig or squirrel than any dog I'd ever seen.

She recounted how she'd found it there, wandering helplessly along the road, and figured maybe I could give it a lift back to the neighborhood.

"Where'd she come from?" I asked, staring out at the endless stretch of fields.

My friend shrugged, said my guess was as good as hers.

I cupped the puppy in my palm and drove her to the cul-de-sac of duplexes that my friend and I called home. I'd hardly stepped from the car when I was greeted by a few of our fellow graduate school writer friends, all of whom wanted to hear the story of the fur ball pressed tight to my chest.

I told them of our friend's rescue mission, how I'd merely served as chauffeur.

The pup's baleful eyes and helpless state tugged at our heartstrings, and though we were just humble graduate students (and thus broke) we still managed to pool together enough money to arrange for a vet visit.

"She's so cute," one friend remarked. "So terribly, terribly cute."

That terribly cute puppy peered up at us adoringly and then proceeded to hack up a pile of writhing worms.

Remarkably, the puppy survived that day, and the day after, and even the day after that. Though in our inexpert opinion she appeared to be just a little over a week old, we were surprised to learn that she was actually well over a month, though so malnourished her true age was masked by her maladies. The vet made the direness of her situation quite clear to us, though she offered a silver lining as well—with the proper treatment, and a good home, our pup could indeed survive.

Within days she began to stage her comeback, finding a home with a pair of neighbors who'd played an active role in her recovery. To this day, Pirl (a name that gives credit to both her pig and squirrel features) continues to be my former neighbors' loyal and faithful dog. Though technically she was a pit bull, when our landlord was present we were always careful to identify her by her formal breed name—American Staffordshire terrier—which was less a lie than a half-truth and imperative to protect Pirl from the breed bias working against her.

Though I've since moved from Alabama, every time I return to that land and reunite with that brown-and-white, barrel-chested dog, I can't help but be reminded how close she came to falling victim to the perils of a country road. And I am reminded also of the callousness of the human that left her there to die — which she would have, had my friend ridden a different route that day.

Why would someone leave her there? I wondered. *What had afforded her that fate?*

Had she been too small, too weak, or simply one of too many in the litter? Or worse, had she just been in the wrong place with the wrong person in the midst of somebody else's bad day?

It's hard to imagine a rationale in which her abandonment made logical sense. Any way I sliced it, leaving a puppy to fend for herself on a kudzu-lined country road seemed an act of cruelty — a trait I once naïvely believed pet owners could not possess.

These days, I know better.

I wish I didn't.

∴

It's not difficult to find a love-struck pet owner; take a doggie biscuit, fling it into the nearest dog park, and you're bound to hit a dozen or two. Far more rare, I hope, is to find a pet owner with hate in his heart. Yet hate alone is not what spurs humans' abuses against animals. Rather, it's often something harder to peg — ambivalence, perhaps, or ignorance.

As I begin my search for lessons that animals might teach us, I decide to put a pin in the animal lovers (I already know them) and focus first on those who may feel otherwise, those who've been known to rule by cruelty or neglect or both.

In my home of Eau Claire, Wisconsin, no one knows these people better than Bekah Weitz.

Though just twenty-eight years old (and having been on the job, officially, for less than a year), Bekah — Eau Claire County's one and only humane officer — already has a keen sense of the people she's dealing with.

"Sometimes I see some terrible things," she warns me in our initial phone conversation, "but if you really want to ride along, well, just know it's not always going to be pretty."

It's with this understanding that I roll to a halt in the Eau Claire County Humane Association's (ECCHA) parking lot a few days later, anxious about—and dreading—the possibility of observing the cruelties that occur in my own backyard.

I step inside the ECCHA building—a no-frills structure just off Interstate 94—and knock on Bekah's closed office door.

From outside, I hear the squeak of her rolling chair, followed by the groan of the door being pulled wide.

"Hey, you must be B.J.," Bekah says, turning her attention from her computer screen. I nod, shake her hand, and thank her for allowing me to ride along for the day.

"No problem," she agrees, returning her attention to the screen. "I'm just trying to figure out our route."

I watch as she types various addresses into Google Maps, creating a gash-like purple line that carves a circle through the county, or at least a small part of it. With a population teetering at just over one hundred thousand, western Wisconsin's Eau Claire County consists of 645 square miles under Bekah's jurisdiction—an impossibly large area for a single humane officer to patrol. Yet Bekah does that to the best of her ability, entering a final address into Google Maps before excusing herself to retrieve the printed copy of our route.

I take a moment to peer around her office, which she shares with another ECCHA employee. It's small, spartan, though homey thanks to the photographs of family and dogs that line Bekah's half of the walls. Beneath the photos are several three-ring binders, each of them filled with the haunting details of the animal-related crimes that have recently occurred in this region.

"Oh, hey, Amber," Bekah calls, returning to her office to greet the twenty-five-year-old blonde woman who has just caught me gawking around the room. "Amber's a veterinary student down in Madison," Bekah explains as she snaps the printed map to her clipboard. "She'll be helping me out today, too."

I smile at Bekah's phrasing, which implies that I, "too," will be of some help to her, though I know better than to believe it. As an animal lover with a weak stomach—I can barely get through Walt Disney's *Homeward Bound: The Incredible Journey* without choking up—I believe myself ill-equipped for the challenges that lie ahead of us. My hope is that I can simply endure the day by serving as the ever-present fly on the wall, listening quietly, intently, and learning as we go.

Waving good-bye to her coworkers, Bekah leads us past a few cats in the front lobby, then directs us to the red pickup with the "I ♥ Dogs" magnet stuck to the tailgate.

Amber settles into the passenger seat while I slip into the back.

"I like driving my pickup," Bekah explains as she fastens the driver-side seat belt, "because when you're driving around rural parts of Wisconsin, you're a lot more inconspicuous this way."

"Do people try to hide from you?" I ask.

"Sometimes," she agrees, slipping on sunglasses, "but the bigger problem is that when they see the shelter van it gives them time to react, especially if they're doing something they're not supposed to be doing. 'Oh, gee, I better hide my puppy mill,'" Bekah says, her voice raising an octave as she tries her best puppy mill breeder impression. "This way," she says, pulling out of the lot, "I can be a little more under the radar."

"A little more covert ops," I agree.

"Exactly," she laughs, "a little more covert ops."

As she fits the GPS to the dash, she assures me she doesn't need the device for navigational purposes but, rather, to assist the police in tracking her location on the off chance she doesn't come back.

"It's always a worry for me," Bekah admits, turning right out of the humane society parking lot and speeding down Old Town Hall Road. "I've been shooting guns since I was five years old, but because I'm a Wisconsin humane officer, I can't carry a gun on duty. So oftentimes I go onto a property blind. And people forget that every type of person owns pets."

"What do you mean?" I ask.

"Pet ownership isn't exclusively for nice people," she explains, confirming what I'd learned after finding Pirl on that rural Alabama road so many years before. "Serial killers own pets, and rapists own pets, and child molesters own pets. Sometimes when I drive up a long driveway out in the country I think, 'Bekah, out here no one could hear you scream.'"

I gulp.

"So anyway," Bekah shrugs, adjusting the small black box as the road materializes onto the screen, "that's why I use a GPS. So if I disappear, they can find my body for my family."

I gulp again.

Bekah Weitz didn't always dream of pursuing the hardened life of a humane officer. Initially, she aspired to be a veterinarian, and if it weren't for the math requirements, she likely would have achieved her goal. Instead, she completed college with a history degree and, soon after, accepted a job at a local chiropractic office. There she whittled away the hours, collected a paycheck, but ultimately found little fulfillment in a job that didn't offer her opportunities to interact with animals.

"It was a good job," Bekah admits. "I had an office and a window and a salary—all the things you're supposed to want. But every day when I was at work I was constantly checking the classifieds. One day I saw that the Eau Claire County Humane Association was hiring. I applied, I got the job, and I immediately learned what it was like to wake up and want to go to work. I was just a kennel attendant back then," she laughs. "I literally just cleaned kennels. But I loved it."

She worked her way up from kennel attendant to adoption coordinator and, finally, to her current position as humane officer. Since 2008 she's worked in her current capacity, though she wasn't officially appointed until 2012, when the job opened up full time.

"I'm always going to conferences and seminars on animal welfare," Bekah says, "but I would say that in this job, nothing trumps experience."

Indeed, she's gained plenty of it—sometimes more than she'd like.

Yet despite her years on the job, her task never becomes easier. Emotionally, it has actually become harder—each animal cruelty case serving to further wear away her optimism about humankind.

"The hardest things to see aren't always cases of neglect. Those are hard, they suck, but so does abject cruelty."

"Abject cruelty?" I ask, peeking my head past the truck's center console toward Bekah and Amber.

"You know," Bekah says as we veer onto Clairemont Avenue, "just the shit people do to be awful human beings."

As she says this, I'm reminded of a trick I learned on the first day of screenwriting class, an old chestnut said to have been used widely throughout the industry: in order to reveal the antagonist to your audience, simply show that person kicking a dog.

The implication is unmistakable, even to the most dimwitted moviegoer. Characters can be complex—and we can often forgive them their trespasses—but no one forgives a dog kicker.

Yet even in the world beyond the silver screen, plenty of people are hurting animals, and more often than not, they're hurting dogs. According to a 2011 report from the Humane Society of the United States, of the 1,880 animal cruelty cases reported in the media in 2007, 64.5 percent involved dogs, 18 percent involved cats, and 25 percent involved all other animals combined (some cases involved multiple species).

Why, I wonder, *does man's so-called best friend bear the greatest burden of our abuses?*

There's no easy answer, primarily because people who treat animals cruelly rarely conform to a single profile. As Bekah knows all too well, instances of animal abuse and neglect occur in both rural and urban settings, at the hands of both rich and poor, black and white, and across other geographic, socioeconomic, and racial barriers. In short, anyone with a temper and a bone to pick might very well choose to pick that bone with an animal.

What we do understand—thanks to a study by Stephen Kellert and Alan Felthous—is that those who abuse animals generally fit into one of nine typologies. To offer but a few: perpetrators' actions are said to be motivated by a desire to control an animal, retaliate (against either an animal or another person), express anger, or redirect anger from a person to an animal, among others. However, perhaps the most troubling typology describes perpetrators who abuse animals for no reason other than to experience sadism firsthand.

This last typology confirms what Bekah had mentioned to me just moments prior: that some people abuse animals just to be awful. It also confirms another of her claims: that pet ownership isn't exclusively for nice people.

For proof, you need only look to some of America's most notorious serial killers. Jeffrey Dahmer, Ted Bundy, and David Berkowitz, among others, all displayed a fascination with performing depraved acts against animals, leading criminal psychologists to believe that these animal abuses foreshadowed their later crimes against humans. As FBI supervisory agent Allen Brantley remarked in an interview, animal cruelty isn't merely a "harmless venting of emotion in a healthy individual" but "a warning sign."

These warning signs extend beyond the world of serial killers to include perpetrators of domestic abuse as well. According to a 1997 joint study between Northeastern University and the Massachusetts Society for the Prevention of Cruelty to Animals, animal abusers are "five times more likely to commit violent crimes against people" than nonabusers are. That same year, a study by Frank Ascione and others further confirmed the connection, reporting that 71 percent of female domestic abuse victims surveyed "indicated that their boyfriend or husband had either threatened harm to their animals or had engaged in actual maltreatment and/or killing of an animal." Though other studies put the percentage slightly lower, the connection between animal abuse and domestic abuse is undeniable. More often than not, people who hurt animals hurt people too.

Fully aware of this connection, Bekah regularly finds herself making phone calls to child protective services as well as other domestic abuse agencies when she uncovers signs of animal abuse.

"Chances are, if someone's of the mind-set that they think they can treat an animal poorly, these people probably aren't going to win parent of the year," she explains. "These things kind of go hand in hand."

Yet on occasion, Bekah explains, the misguided pet owner acts out in an attempt to "protect" the family and, whether the perpetrator realizes it or not, exhibits several of Kellert and Felthous's typologies in the process.

"Probably the worst case I ever had involved this one guy," she begins. "His dog, his family dog—this twelve-year-old golden retriever—apparently bit his kid. From what I could tell, it was a total accident. The dog was lying on the ground, fast asleep, and the kid just fell on it. So the dog woke up, turned its head, and kind of bit at the child. It wasn't an evil dog. It was a good dog," Bekah says, glancing in the rearview while switching lanes. "Anyway, as a result of the bite, the man beat his dog to death with a shovel."

My heart sinks, and though I can't imagine the story getting any worse, it does.

"The thing that was really sad wasn't just that he killed his dog, but that when I went out there to investigate it, the dog didn't have any sort of indication on her body that she'd tried to get away. He had tied her up and beat her to death with a shovel, so normally you'd see ligature marks around the collar when she tried to run. But there were none, which means she just stood there. *That* was the sad part," Bekah says, her eyes hidden behind her shades. "Not that he killed her, but that she let him."

∴

Too often we hear stories of loyalty gone bad; it happens in the human world as well. While it's likely an overreach to consider Bekah's gut-wrenching anecdote as describing the animal equivalent to Stockholm syndrome, I can't help but link the two in my head. We pet owners prefer not to think of ourselves as our animals' "captors," though we do dictate virtually every aspect of their lives (not to mention that most of our dictating is scheduled around our own lives). "Human

companion" is a far easier phrase to swallow and, in fact, is the preferred term for many of the more progressive pet owners among us.
Yet even though I fancy myself my dog Cici's human companion, I
am also her owner, and perhaps her captor, too. After all, I purchased
her and she is licensed to me. Legally, she is my property. That I care
for her the best I can is certainly important, though I'm not sure this
changes the status of our relationship. Examining how pet owners/
captors/companions self-identify surely provides some insight into
their views on their relationship with their animals, but how are we
to take the animal's opinion into consideration? Do we test their
loyalties by flinging the doors wide and watching what happens next?
Conversely, to those who argue that pet ownership is in itself a form
of abuse, isn't abandonment equally cruel?

These are the complications Bekah mulls over as she takes a slurp of
coffee, folds a stick of gum into her mouth, then cranks up the Nirvana
song on the radio. By the time the song finishes, we've arrived in the
nearby town of Clear Creek, population 712, so Bekah can follow up
on a report of an unhealthily thin horse.

"There's a chance I know this horse," Bekah says as we barrel down
the road together. She leans forward as she begins scanning addresses,
though we spot the horse long before the mailbox. "Oh yeah, I know
this one," she agrees, pulling to the side of the road and reaching for
her clipboard. "But these folks are really good people. They get called
in a couple times a year because they have this, like, thirty-eight-year-
old horse," she says, jotting down a few notes. "Sometimes people
report what they think is a starving horse, but really they're confusing
it with an old horse. And in this case," she says, putting the truck back
into drive, "we're just looking at an old horse."

"You're a regular Dr. Doolittle," I say. "You know all the animals,
down to some random horse in a random pasture in a random
town . . ."

"Well, it's not that random," she admits. "I know this horse because
it's been called in before. But it's true: in this job, you do get to know

the animals, and the people, too, which is sometimes depressing. When I'm out driving around I can't help but think, 'That guy killed his dog,' or 'That woman starved her cat.' I guess everyone's got a story."

Indeed, and Bekah Weitz appears to know all of them. Even though I've spent little more than an hour with her, it's already clear she's made it her business to know the business of seemingly every at-risk animal in the county.

As Bekah explains, her job doesn't end with the animals; it's important for her to know their people as well. To this end, she maintains a carefully documented history of alleged animal abuse. Over time, Bekah has accrued a manila file for each of her cases, and as she uncaps the pen and makes another note, I can't help but feel as if I'm watching a one-woman show, which, to some extent, I am. While the city of Eau Claire has a few animal control officers on the payroll, the county—which covers a far greater area—has Bekah alone. Yet despite being outnumbered and overworked, she isn't one to complain.

Even when I ask her to describe a normal day, she does so matter-of-factly.

"Well, last night I got home from work at 6:30, and I was still on the phone with people until around 9:30. Then I was up this morning at 6:00 working," she tells me.

"That seems well beyond the normal nine to five," I say.

"Yeah," she says, "but I do it because I'm the only one who can do a lot of this stuff, and you just got to do it, just got to get it done."

"Somebody's got to," I agree.

"Shelter workers are the same way," she adds. "They don't have to be at work until 8:30, but there were people at the shelter at 7:00 this morning to let dogs out and dispense medication. And it's also the beginning of kitten season." She smiles knowingly. "Amber's got some foster kittens, don't you, Amber?"

"I do," Amber agrees.

"Pretty much everyone's got some foster kittens right now, actually,"

Bekah laughs. "But that's how we are. We get to work early, we stay late, and we don't necessarily get paid for it because the shelter can't afford it. Sometimes people clock out but just stay there."

"So let me get this straight," I begin, "you put yourself at risk, work long hours, and witness horrible cruelties wrought upon animals day after day. All for what exactly?"

"Well, because we have to," Bekah says, driving us deeper into the country, "because no one else will."

She pauses, considers her statement, then backpedals.

"It's not that *no one else will*, it's that *I* will. And that Sara, our adoption coordinator, will. And that Tammy and Liz and Todd all will. We *can* do it, and we know we *should* do it, so we *do* it."

Amber shoots a quick smile toward Bekah, and it's hard for me not to shoot her one myself. There's something quite motivating about spending time with a person who loves her devastatingly difficult job, though by the same token, it's frustrating to see just how underappreciated she is, at least monetarily. After all, Bekah performs a job I wouldn't do for any amount of money, and yet she does it irrespective of her modest hourly wage. On average, animal control officers in Wisconsin earn $25,350 per year—making the state forty-fourth in compensation for animal control workers—but Bekah does it for far less. In fact, according to Bekah, she's the lowest-paid member of law enforcement in the county, with a salary just beneath that of parking attendants.

"Now don't get me wrong," Bekah continues. "It sucks. The pay is awful. The hours are horrible. The mental fatigue that you suffer is absolutely unbearable sometimes. There's not a single person who works at the shelter who I don't think has trouble with compassion fatigue. This is the kind of job that gives you nightmares."

She explains that an unintended side effect of working in the animal welfare field is that the mental anguish often leads people to substance abuse.

"It's almost like PTSD," she confesses. "You have to work through it. Or at the very least you've got to develop a hobby. Find something in your life that has nothing to do with animals. Find some way for you to unwind."

"Have you found your way to unwind?"

She nods, tells me she used to perform in Renaissance fairs.

"We did unarmed combat in the streets," she says. "It was supposed to look spontaneous. Like, we'd pretend to play cards, someone would cheat, and then we'd do all these choreographed acrobatics. We didn't use swords. Just fisticuffs," she laughs. "But I stopped doing that about two years ago. Now—and I know this is horribly nerdy—I play *Dungeons and Dragons* with friends. Everyone's got to have something."

"We talk about this in vet school all the time," Amber adds. "How, when you look at statistics, people in the veterinary field have one of the highest rates of suicide."

Not *one* of the highest, but *the* highest, at least according to veterinarian and doctoral student David Bartram and professor of psychiatry David Baldwin's 2010 journal article, "Veterinary Surgeons and Suicides: A Structured Review of Possible Influences on Increased Risk." The article reveals that British vets are four times as likely as the general public to commit suicide, giving veterinary medicine "far and away the highest suicide rate of any other occupational group." Potential causes of the abnormally high suicide rate vary, though they are often attributed to the stressful work environment, one that demands "long hours, high psychological demands, low level of support from managers and high expectations from clients." Factor in veterinarians' close proximity to lethal drugs, as well as the cognitive dissonance felt by those whose moral views on euthanasia are at odds with their task, and suddenly we on the outside begin to better understand the untenable pressures felt almost exclusively by vets.

While some U.S. veterinarians find it unlikely that Bartram and Baldwin's study of their British counterparts accurately reflects their own experience, others, like Chicago's Michele Gaspar, fully believe there is reason for concern, that the combination of high stress and easy access to barbiturates places vets in a uniquely dangerous position. Speaking to a crowd of first-year veterinary students, Gaspar remarked, "In . . . some ways, the very traits that will make you dedicated veterinarians — including your passion and compassion — can also make you more vulnerable."

Bekah and other shelter employees are susceptible to many of the same risks. They, too, work long hours in stressful environments and must also bear the burden of euthanizing the very animals they strive to protect.

"Being a euth tech's a heavy job when you work at the shelter," Bekah says. "You really have to get your head straight or you can go the wrong way really quick. There's not a month that goes by that I'm not killing the animals I love."

Doing so often comes with a psychological cost, one Bekah has paid dearly for.

One afternoon a few months earlier, Bekah had found herself sitting atop a bag of dog food in the shelter, overwhelmed by a particularly daunting case. Uncertain of whom to call for help, she reached for her cell phone and tried the sergeant at the Eau Claire sheriff's department, who was also working the case, and left him a message.

"Hi," she said to his voicemail, "I'm just calling you because I don't know who else to call. I need some help."

The following morning, the sergeant pulled into the shelter lot to spend some time with Bekah. Together they processed evidence in the lockup room, as well as swapped a few war stories.

"I was overwhelmed," Bekah admits. "Not by anything I didn't know how to do. It was just . . . what was before me was immense. And I have a bad habit of looking at the top of the mountain and not focusing my eyes on the trail that leads me there."

The pair chatted until Bekah began to regain her footing and continued moving up the mountaintop. By the time the sergeant waved good-bye, Bekah knew she'd called the right person.

"Law enforcement, like animal welfare, has a lot of burnout. The sergeant knows that, and I know that. Sometimes you go home and don't have anything you can do or say to make yourself feel better.

You just think, 'This horrible thing has happened and I can't fix it, and I can't make it better, and I can't kill myself tonight because if I do, no one will be able to do my job tomorrow . . .'"

Bekah—whose dark shades and leather jacket project a tough front—is momentarily beside herself. Her "don't screw with me" persona subsides, and from my place in the backseat of her truck, I'm left peering at the corners of her eyes, otherwise hidden behind those glasses.

"Every time there's a thunderstorm I think of all the dogs tied to trees with no shelter," she begins. "And when it snows I wonder who's freezing to death . . . I'm always wondering who I missed, who I don't know about."

She hesitates before continuing.

"There's a horse less than a mile from my house that starved to death before I managed to save her pasture mate. That killed me. Less than a mile from my house a horse starved to death and I didn't even know."

"It's sort of you versus the world," I observe, peering out at the miles upon miles of country roads that sprawl ahead of us.

She shrugs, just keeps driving.

∵

Twenty minutes later we arrive in the village of Fairchild.

"Okay," Bekah says, double-checking an address against her notes, "we got a report about a skinny pit bull that lives here. So now we'll just go ahead and see what's going on."

I unbuckle my seat belt and join Bekah and Amber outside. It's a perfect June morning, blue skies overhead and plush grass beneath our shoes. Birds chirp, chimes ring, and the pristine landscape stretching before me seems to distract from any signs of animal abuse.

How, I wonder, *could something terrible ever happen here?*

Like a pair of untrained bodyguards, Amber and I flank Bekah as she knocks sharply on the door.

Rap-rap-rap.

We wait.

Nothing.

She tries again—*rap-rap-rap*—but still, nobody comes to answer us. As we turn to leave, we hear barking coming from the yard.

"Plain-sight doctrine means I can only take evidence if it's in plain sight," Bekah says as we walk toward the porch, "but since this is the porch and it's in plain sight . . ."

Suddenly, a dog appears before us.

"Hi, boy," Bekah calls to the dog, her voice raising a few octaves. "You're not a pit bull, are ya?" she coos. "You're a collie."

The dog—who could pass for Lassie's stunt double—barks in reply. I breathe a sigh of relief. Not only does it look as if we've been momentarily spared a confrontation with a pet owner, but if any of us happen to fall into a nearby well, our Lassie lookalike appears ready and willing to save us.

Reaching for her camera, Bekah snaps a few evidential photos of the dog. Though my own outward examination leads me to believe that we're looking at one healthy collie, Bekah informs me that when investigating cases of cruelty and neglect, one must always remember to look beyond the dog and at the dog's living conditions as well.

"He may not have adequate food and water out there," Bekah says, craning her neck in search of a bowl that might fall within our sights. "In fact, he might not have adequate shelter, either."

Providing the essentials—food, water, and shelter—is the minimum responsibility of pet ownership. Ensuring only that your animal has access to these basic and fundamental necessities may not win you the admiration of a pet-loving populace, but barring any visible scars on your animal, it will also likely ensure that Bekah won't have a manila file with your name on it. However, if Bekah were to arrive at your home to find a skinny, panting animal baking in the sun, chances are you'd have to worry about more than a manila file. And while Bekah would certainly hear you out, I'm willing to wager no storyteller could spin a yarn that would allow these trespasses to go unpunished.

Bekah snaps a few final photos of the dog, then pulls a yellow door tag from her clipboard and scribbles a note asking the pet owner to give her a call.

"Do people call you back?" I ask.

"If they don't I just come back out and bug them again," Bekah shrugs, wedging the tag between screen door and door. "We'll chat one way or another."

From behind us, we hear a few more barks from the collie.

"Hi, sweetie, you're very pretty," Bekah smiles.

Another few barks.

"I know, and I'm sorry," Bekah says as we head back toward the truck. "But don't worry, girl, I'll be back soon."

∵

We barrel northwest for seven miles, eventually pulling to the side of the road in Augusta, a small city to the southeast of Eau Claire. Though I now know the general routine (get out of the truck, put on a brave face, and knock sharply on the door), since we've yet to interact with a human, my nerves remain on edge. After all, we're not exactly selling Girl Scout cookies here. Instead, we're marching onto people's properties to question their ability to adequately care for their animals. Depending on the pet owners' answers (as well as Bekah's observations), we are then charged (well, Bekah is charged) with determining whether to seize the animal from the home. It likely comes as no surprise that pet owners aren't always thrilled with Bekah's determinations, nor do situations always go as planned. Though our previous stops had ended rather anti-climactically, I know it's just a matter of time before we reach our climax.

As I slip from the truck, my eye catches the GPS on the dash.

Don't worry, I think, *if things go south, at least they'll find our bodies.*

My heart nearly thumps from my chest as Bekah knocks on the door, though when a docile-looking elderly man answers, my heart rate returns to a medically healthy range.

I wait for the badass version of Bekah to emerge and raise hell toward this alleged animal abuser, though the badass version never makes an appearance. Not in the least. Though her dark glasses and leather jacket ensemble seem appropriate for any card-carrying Hell's Angel, Bekah's dress hardly matches her demeanor.

"Hi, there," she says, greeting the man with a grin. "I'm Bekah, the humane officer for Eau Claire County. I got a call that you had some dogs that are maybe a bit skinny."

"Nope," the man says, reaching for the door.

"Do you own dogs?"

"Yes," he admits.

"Can I take a look at your dogs?"

The elderly man shoots his wife a look before relenting.

"All right," he sighs, opening the storm door wide for us.

We've hardly stepped inside before being greeted by the couple's overzealous dachshund.

"Hi, there," Bekah says, focusing first on the dog, then the owner. "He's cute."

The elderly man's wife joins us, and together, the five of us stand around the living room as we discuss the dog's condition.

Once more, I see no signs of abuse, neglect, or cruelty, and this time, Bekah seems to agree. The dachshund appears to be of a normal, healthy weight, but Bekah has other concerns, mainly the couple's inability to identify their vet.

"We have to get money for that," the woman eventually admits.

The dachshund scrambles past me toward the door and tries to nose his way out. I redirect him, listening to his skittering claws tear against the wooden floors.

"Well, he looks real healthy," Bekah agrees. "Why don't I give you my card?"

Ignoring her, the elderly man turns to his wife and says, "Get the chain."

She does, and the man snaps the dog to the leash, then drags the dachshund past me and out the door.

"I'll never get this dog under control," the man mutters as the storm door slams behind him—a complaint I've muttered myself on dozens of occasions.

Bekah and the woman chat for a few minutes more, and as we turn to take our leave, the woman reiterates the same message she's been spouting since we first walked through her door.

"He's not skinny," she insists. "Our dog isn't skinny."

"Yes, ma'am," Bekah agrees. "Let me just give you my card."

As we step outside, we're greeted by the clip-clop of a horse and buggy, a white-bearded Amish man working the reins. He smiles and waves—his animal in complete control—while a few yards away, the elderly man and his dachshund take turns dragging one another through the tall grass. I wave good-bye, and the man returns the wave, then speeds up to keep his dog from strangling himself.

"So that's it?" I ask as we step inside the truck. "That's all we do for now?"

Bekah nods.

Perhaps my desire for decisive action is the result of having watched one too many cop shows, though as Bekah teaches me, building a case takes time. Likewise, without proof of abuse, all we can do is make a note in a manila file—which Bekah does, before opening her center console. Inside, I spot a Prodigy CD and, just beneath, a small bottle of hand sanitizer. She reaches for the bottle, squirts a healthy glob into her palm, then passes it back to me.

"A piece of advice," she says as she rubs her hands together. "If you touch a dog, use hand sanitizer. It's even the sparkly kind."

"Even better," I smile, squirting a small pool into my own hands before passing the bottle to Amber.

"Oh, and here's another piece of advice," Bekah says as she puts the truck in drive. "If you ever take a job where you wear a badge, always eat at a place where you can watch them make your food. Just trust me on that."

Amber and I chuckle.

Five minutes later, we park in front of a Subway.

⠒

The afternoon passes quickly, proof of our long day apparent only in Bekah's case notes and the eighty or so miles clocked on the truck's odometer. We briefly investigate a few other complaints (nothing to write home about) before dedicating the majority of our time to a claim of some unhealthy cattle just outside of town.

Over lunch, Bekah had explained to me that accusing someone of being an irresponsible pet owner is often viewed as "a slap in the face." And so, after she parks the truck alongside a farmhouse, I am hardly surprised to lock eyes with a man who appears to brace himself for a slap.

Escorted by a jaunty German shepherd, the three of us approach the farmer.

"Hi there," Bekah begins, "we got a call about some skinny cattle."

My eyes go immediately to the gun holstered on the man's hip.

Well, I think, *I suppose we've reached our climax.*

I'm nervous, sweaty, and for a moment, find myself wondering just how accurate that GPS really is.

Bekah doesn't flinch, which makes me wonder if she sees it or if she's simply grown accustomed to the threat of violence.

"You mind if I go take a look at them?" Bekah asks, nodding to the pasture.

"Okay," the man agrees, offering not a single word more than is required of him. Bekah takes the lead, followed by Amber, then the farmer, then his dog, and finally, me.

"They're out there eating right now," the farmer says, following us down the grassy hill to the edge of the fence. "They're just finishing up the bale."

After a pause he asks, "Are we allowed to know who called us in?"

"You know, I don't have a name on it," Bekah says.

I can't tell if she's lying or not.

"Well, that figures," the farmer grumbles.

Bekah continues her visual observation, implementing the

plain-sight doctrine for all it is worth. She scans the four or five head of cattle milling about in the pasture, keeping a close eye on their ribs and their hooves.

"Do you feed round or square bales?" she asks.

"Round," the man says.

"These all beef?"

"Yup."

"You don't have any dairy?"

"Lord God, no, I don't want anything to do with them."

Bekah and Amber laugh at his apparent joke, though my own timid laughter pegs me as the city slicker.

"Dairy cows are a lot of work," Bekah explains, then turns her attention to a pair of horses in an adjacent pen. "Mind if I go take a look at your horses?"

"Go ahead," the man agrees, seeming to have warmed to us, at least a little.

While the cattle appear to be fine, Bekah notes a few concerns about the horses' hooves.

"Can I get your phone number," Bekah asks, "so I can call you back?"

After a pause, the man eventually relents.

"Great, I'll give you a call back about the horses," she says.

And then, to lessen the blow: "But you're right—those cattle don't look like they're having any trouble. They've got food and water and . . ."

"Beefcakes!" the man hollers, suddenly proud to show off his herd.

The word hardly leaves his mouth before the cattle—the "Beef-cakes"—tilt their heads up from the grass and begin lumbering toward us. "Come on now, Beefcakes," he repeats.

Even I understand this joke.

"Yeah, they're looking good," Bekah repeats, offering the man the assurance he's after before returning to the real problem. "And like I said, I'll give you a call if I need to get in touch about the horses."

"I wouldn't know why you'd have to," the man says, growing

defensive once more as he walks toward the pen and rubs a hand against his Belgian.

"You're so hungry," he jokes to his horse. "Just wasting away. I don't know how you even survive."

What he fails to understand is that Bekah isn't concerned about the horses' weight, but their hooves, that caring for horses requires more than food and water.

"Thanks for taking the time to talk to us," Bekah calls, ignoring the sarcasm as we step back into the truck.

"Sure," he agrees.

Before we drive off the property, he calls out to us once more.

"Whoever called us in has no idea what they're talking about," he claims.

Us, I think as I watch the horses, cattle, dog, and man fade in the rearview. *Us.*

∴

By 3:00 p.m., we return to Bekah's office.

"You mind entering these into the computer?" Bekah asks, handing Amber a stack of files. Amber agrees, waves good-bye, then leaves Bekah and me to reflect on our day.

"I told you it wouldn't be pretty," she says. I agree, though I'm also grateful it wasn't any worse. With the exception of my glancing the gun holstered on the farmer's hip, the ride along had been a bit less dramatic than I expected. But in Bekah's business, drama is best left to the movies.

In real life, the dramatic stories are often too horrible even to put on the page. Certainly I don't want to hear of them; likely you don't, either. Suffice it to say, if an act seems unthinkably cruel, chances are, some human has thought to carry it out, particularly on an animal. Which is why people like Bekah are so important to ensure that animals are afforded a basic level of dignity and respect—a lesson that applies to humans as well.

"One thing that always appalls me is that when we realize an animal is being raised for food, we treat it as such until it's butchered," Bekah says. "But being able to look into the future and see when and where and how that animal will die doesn't mean that its life prior to that moment need be horrific."

I nod.

"We live like we expect to live forever, and I think that's really at the core of why we humans have a hard time with our own mortality. We can't face it because if we face it, we feel like our life isn't worth living well," she explains. "If we know that this steer will be butchered in two years, we feel like we don't need him to live well either, because we know he's going to die. He seems hopeless to us. And we humans aren't comfortable feeling hopeless. We much prefer to live our lives with hope."

It's simple yet powerful. How often have we all sought out silver linings amid sadness, manufacturing a modicum of hope in situations that otherwise appeared hopeless? Hope implies a fighting chance, a fair shake, the possibility for improvement. Conversely, to live without hope is to admit defeat, to acknowledge that nothing you say or do will have an impact on anything. And if people like Bekah choose to embrace this credo, what's the point in trying?

"Thanks, Bekah," I say. "For everything."

"No problem," she shrugs, flashing me the briefest smile before her eyes zero in on the computer screen. The sound of her typing serenades me back to the parking lot, at which point I plop into the driver's seat of my car. I'm exhausted, but not defeated. How could I be, given what I've learned?

Amid a chorus of barks and yowls from the dogs in the outside pen, I scribble my first pet-inspired lesson into my notebook, one I'm not soon to forget:

LESSON #1: LIVE YOUR LIFE WITH HOPE.

TWO

OLD DOGS, NEW SHTICKS

Blessed is the person who has earned the love of an old dog.

— SYDNEY JEANNE SEWARD

In 1996 my mother, father, brother, and I wandered into the local branch of the Society for the Prevention of Cruelty to Animals in search of the perfect dog. We had a pretty good idea what we wanted: something wet-nosed and furry and fun. But what we also knew—even if we never acknowledged it aloud—was that what we really wanted was a puppy.

Why did we have our hearts set on a puppy? For the same reasons so many others do: because puppies are playful and cute, and because a puppy will spend her entire life with you, thus forming a closer bond with her human family.

At least that's what we thought.

Indeed, puppies *are* playful and puppies *are* cute, but they don't hold the exclusive rights to these attributes. Older dogs play as well, and their version of play usually ends with far fewer slobber-soaked slippers. As for cuteness, though some older dogs may outgrow the term, other terms easily replace it. Old dogs are regal, wise, worldly, and intuitive, and they, too, can be easy on the eyes. As to the charge that young dogs create stronger bonds with their people, anecdotal evidence seems to point to the contrary. In a world in which loyalty and love are often linked, it's misguided to presume that elderly dogs — dogs with the most experience in these areas — are somehow too enfeebled to form a bond. We aren't asking them to leap hurdles, after all, merely to nuzzle their way into our hearts.

It's a skill at which senior dogs have become highly adept; just ask Amy Quella, whose own heart has been both broken and healed by her dogs. Following the 2005 death of Bob — she and her husband Travis's beloved Eskimo mix — the couple found themselves at a grief-stricken crossroad. Amy had just lost her mother, Travis his father, but losing Bob served as the final push toward a bold reexamination of their lives. Though Amy and Travis had toyed with the idea of creating some kind of dog adoption facility, they'd always deferred that dream for retirement. Yet after losing Bob, they realized their dream could not wait.

We've got to do something now, Amy told herself. *We can't wait any longer.*

For the previous sixteen years, Amy had dedicated her life to a career as a dental assistant, and while she enjoyed the work, it didn't fulfill her on a deeper level. She wanted something more, something to help her heal the scar that Bob had left. The only question that remained was how best to honor Bob's memory.

The answer soon became clear: give homeless dogs a home.

And not just any old homeless dogs, mind you, but *old* homeless dogs — those with the slimmest chance of finding a home elsewhere.

What we need to create, Amy realized, *is a place where senior dogs can flourish.*

Which is exactly what the Quellas did.

Situated just a few miles south of Eau Claire, Bob's House for Dogs currently serves as the region's only foster care facility dedicated exclusively to senior dogs. Think of it as the human equivalent of a retirement community, only with fewer golf carts and Hawaiian shirts and quite a bit more barking. Though Bob's House isn't the first of its kind, it's part of a growing trend, one that has found success in places like Cleveland and San Francisco and Chicago. I'm hardly surprised to learn that senior dog facilities exist, though I am surprised one is located just a fifteen-minute drive from my home.

Eight years after the Quellas first dreamed of this place, I step from my car and peer out at their dream come to fruition: a red-roofed, one-story structure situated directly behind Amy and Travis's personal residence. Judging by the exterior, Bob's House appears fit for any human, though it's not for us; it's a place, quite literally, gone to the dogs.

I step from the car, then turn toward the sound of a van pulling up the long, country drive. In the driver's seat, a silhouetted woman waves to me, smiles, then parks near the back of the lot. Out steps the dark-haired, forty-two-year-old Amy, sweat glistening beneath the brim of her blue Nike hat.

"You must be B.J.," she says, stepping from the van, dog in tow. "Well, come on in, let us show you around."

There it is again—us—the carefully selected pronoun that even the gun-toting farmer had used when describing himself and his "Beef-cakes." I want to linger on this detail, ask Amy about the moment in her life when "me" became "us," when singular became plural, when the lone wolf found her pack. But since it's just one of the many questions swirling around my head, I decide to start us off with an easier one.

"So where'd you two just get back from?" I ask, hustling after them as we head toward the front door to Bob's house.

"We had a home visit."

"How'd it go?"

"Great," Amy says, tousling the elderly dog's white fur. "He made a great little match with Ernie, the shih tzu that already lives at the house."

"You do home visits," I say, impressed. "You're a full-service shelter."

"Oh, I think you'll find we're a little different than a shelter," she says, placing a hand on the doorknob and turning to face me. "You sure you're ready for this?"

"Sure," I say. "I think so."

"Okay, then," Amy calls, flinging the door wide. "Welcome to Bob's House."

No trumpets herald our arrival, just twenty-eight-year-old Nikki Ristau, the facilities manager, alongside a dozen or so exuberant dogs. I try introducing myself to Nikki, but the chorus of yips, howls, and rattling collars makes it impossible for my voice to carry even the short distance between us.

I enter through the next layer of security—a doggie gate—and sink to my knees, a position that ensures I am soon overwhelmed by a never-ending supply of dog kisses. Suddenly I am covered in so many rough tongues and wet snouts that I can hardly even open my eyes.

"Okay, introductions," Amy says, taking inventory of her dogs. "We've got Petunia and Shadow over there, and Izzy's the little beagle. Rose is the one snoozing on Felix, Warren's our hospice dog, and then we've got the German shepherds—Bear, Scooter, and Midnight . . ."

I try nodding my head—an action made all the more difficult by the sixty or so paws kneading every square inch of my body. Everyone here demands a belly rub, though I only have so many hands.

"They act like they don't get any attention," Amy scoffs as I come up for air. "You're so neglected, huh, guys?"

They belt out their answer in howls.

How, I wonder as I'm swarmed by the dogs, *could I have imagined that a puppy could bond better than this?*

These dogs appear well seasoned in sharing love, and since they aren't in short supply of it, they dole it out generously. Yet beyond all the usual behavior I've come to expect from dogs (barking, licking, crotch sniffing), these senior dogs offer me additional insight into their unique personalities: tap dancing and moonwalking and spinning tight circles in search of a tail. To my left, one head butts another like a mountain goat, while just ahead, another rolls belly up and tears at the air. On the drive over, I wasn't sure what to expect—a pack of geriatric, mottled fur snoozers, perhaps—though upon entering Bob's House, my assumptions are immediately proved wrong. These dogs are frenetic, sliding across the concrete floors like bumper cars on ice.

As I rub as many bellies as possible, Amy runs me through their ages (most of them ten and up), though none of the dogs seem to know it.

When I finally manage to bring my head above the fur line, I'm amazed at the house stretched before me. For the most part, it resembles any other house — complete with couches and a bathtub and artwork lining the walls — though there are a few pragmatic modifications to accommodate the elderly animals' needs, most notably, the urine-resistant concrete floors. All in all, it wouldn't be a bad place for humans to live, as long as they didn't mind fifteen to twenty overly friendly housemates.

Bob's House's current population sits steadily at seventeen — dogs of all ages and breeds that somehow still manage to keep their place far cleaner than my old college roommate and I ever could. Though Bob's House's tidiness is indeed remarkable given the gallons of urine that pass through these bladders daily, even more exciting to me is the implicit argument hidden within its walls. By its very existence, Bob's House for Dogs provides potential pet adopters of this region an opportunity to rethink their options.

Sure, you may think *you want a puppy*, Amy often tells people, *but have you considered the benefits of adopting a senior dog?*

At most shelters, this can be a tough sell. After all, barring some enormous and unexpected cultural shift, puppies are likely to remain the pick of the litter for quite some time to come. But what happens when one creates a puppy-free zone? When one levels the pet adoption playing field to ensure that veterans are never forced to compete against the rookies? At Bob's House, senior dogs are always the first to find homes because they are the only dogs available. When prospective adopters step foot inside Bob's House, they're greeted exclusively by a pack of playful old pooches (none of whom, I might add, are stingy with their kisses).

"So how does all of this happen?" I ask, marveling at the building's interior. "How do you build a house for dogs?"

Amy explains that construction began in December 2009, when, with the help of several friends, she and her husband poured the foundation on what would one day become the structure we're standing in now.

Each friend volunteered his or her expertise—framing, wiring, plumbing—and by year's end, the Quellas' dream had come true.

This teamwork approach has proved equally successful in other senior dog adoption centers throughout the country. In 2007 Sherri Franklin—proverbially known as the "fairy godmother to senior dogs"—enlisted the support of local attorneys and grant writers to assist her in creating Muttville, a San Francisco–based senior dog facility now known nationally for its high adoption rates. In its first year, Muttville and its fifteen volunteers rescued 27 senior dogs, though by its second year, the number of dogs leapt to 198. Three years after its founding, Franklin had amassed a volunteer army over two hundred strong, creating a snowball effect that led to a whopping 408 adoptions in 2012. Franklin's success has garnered Muttville media attention from *Oprah* on down, which has done much to draw further attention to the plight of senior dogs everywhere.

The story of Muttville is inspirational indeed, though so is the story of Bob's House. After all, the Quellas' real-life drama has all the makings of a Hollywood blockbuster: tragedy, adversity, followed by the dream come true.

"So I understand why this place was built," I say, taking a knee to pet a few nearby dogs. "But what I don't understand is *how*. How do you pay for it? How does a nonprofit pay for a house, and a yard, and vet bills? Not to mention a couple of tons of dog food . . ."

Amy smiles, lowering her hands and allowing the dogs to sneak in for a lick.

"A good chunk of the money was part of an inheritance when my father passed away," Amy explains, "and then right off the bat we had to start fundraising."

Much of the funding comes as a result of Bruisin' for Bob's House—an annual three-mile adventure race complete with mud pits, tire mountains, slip-n-slides, and hammer throws, among a dozen or so other obstacles. It's an event I'll take part in myself three months later, enduring the heat and the mud and a bee sting or two, all for the good of the dogs. Yet the obstacles I'll face are far less daunting than trying to maintain the Quellas' $130,000 annual operating budget. As one might expect, sheltering and feeding up to one hundred senior dogs each year certainly isn't cheap, and the Quellas' greatest expense comes in the form of X-rays, blood tests, and teeth cleanings, among other veterinary-related procedures, all of which add up to well over $1,000 a month.

"We've really sacrificed a lot of our own money, too," Amy admits. "Ninety-five thousand dollars or so."

But she's hardly deterred by the price tag. In fact, the ability to see the dogs beyond their vet bills is an attribute Amy demands from all her potential adopters.

"When people look at an older dog, they start thinking about all the medical attention they might need," Amy explains. "They see dollar signs and nothing more. I want people to see more."

However, vet bills are indeed a reality, and something to be considered by any potential pet owner, especially someone intent on adopting a senior dog. According to the American Pet Products Association, in 2013 vet care costs exceeded $14 billion, second only to food in terms of pet-related expenses. The Eau Claire County Humane Association estimates that between $100 and $300 should be budgeted annually for vet bills, a reality that has deterred at least a few potential pet owners. Add to this the cost of food ($24/month), treats ($10/month), heartworm prevention ($40–$65/year), flea and tick prevention ($70/year), grooming, boarding, and toys, as well as a multitude of unforeseen expenses (the new pair of slippers, the slobber-soaked library book, etc.), and the price tag for owning a dog continues to soar. All of these peripheral expenses should be expected, but far too often, potential pet owners see the one-time adoption fee and fail to consider all future expenses, a mistake somewhat equivalent to purchasing a car without budgeting for the gas.

Though Bob's House has no adoption fees, the shelters for which they foster dogs ask for between $100 and $300 — coincidentally, the exact price range estimated for a year's worth of vet care.

Thus, when adopting a pet, it's best to consider the adoption a commitment no different than marriage — for better, for worse, for richer, for poorer, in sickness and in health, for as long as your pet shall live.

∴

Amy walks me through the living room until we reach a rear exit just off the back of the house.

"We call this the big dog litter box," Amy jokes, opening the door and leading us — all ten of us — into a gravel play area.

"Watch where you step," Amy warns, nodding to a few fresh piles accumulating near the edges of the chain-link fence. But aside from the doggie business (and judging by the number of piles, these dogs appear to be captains of industry), the backyard of Bob's House — including a fenced corridor connecting the litter box to an acre-long dog run in the Quellas' backyard — exceeds my expectations. Maybe it's the hand nuzzling, or the tail wagging, or the breeze wafting through the chimes, but for whatever reason, as I peer down at the dogs leisurely sunning themselves at my feet, I feel as if I've stumbled into dog heaven.

Not only does it look like dog heaven, but the animals behave in a manner befitting the place. Throughout my hour and a half at Bob's House, I hear no snarls and see no curled upper lips. There are plenty of yips, of course (directly followed by a few decibel-shattering barks), but all the banter is offered in good, nonthreatening fun. No one bothers anyone. Instead, every dog simply minds his or her own business (again, watch your step), and appears to be having a howling good time.

Yet prior to taking part in this good time, many of the dogs at Bob's House must first adjust to their temporary home. And for many, this adjustment is anything but easy. Though no one path leads dogs to Bob's House, Amy has found that most of these paths are lined with heartbreak. After all, what kinds of pet owners break their vows in the twilight of a pet's life?

The answer: those with little choice.

When the recession hit in 2008, people lost not only their homes and their livelihoods, but on occasion, even their pets. When Americans could hardly afford to put food on their tables, they had a hard time filling dog and cat bowls as well. In 2009 National Public Radio's *All Things Considered* reported on these "foreclosure pets," quoting Dawn Lauer of the Humane Society of the United States, who remarked that "the toll on pets is just as big as on people," adding also that pet relinquishment rates had increased as a result of the fiscal crisis. As proof, NPR turned to Peggy Weigle, the executive director of Animal Humane New Mexico, who confirmed a 400 percent increase in animal intakes at her shelter between 2007 and 2008. The recession's effects on people and their pets became so widespread that the Humane Society of the United States created a Foreclosure Pets Fund to provide financial assistance for shelters and animal rescue clinics, which in turn employed the funds to assist pet owners directly. As the recession dragged into 2009 and 2010, the newly constructed Bob's House began receiving its own pack of foreclosure pets.

Economics, however, isn't the only reason people become separated from their pets. A pet owner's lifestyle changes can also spark the split. One of the most common involves the birth of a new child, which—while thrilling to the parents—can severely complicate a pet's position in the household. When preparing to bring our son Henry home from the hospital, I did everything I could to prepare Cici for the transition, including sharing Henry's onesie with her in an attempt to familiarize her with his scent. When we brought him home two days later, she was ready for him and, in fact, grew so excited that she began shaking uncontrollably—an act I quite optimistically chalked up as pure, unadulterated joy.

For days, she perched atop the arm of the couch and peered down into his crib. She was curious, sure, but also protective, and my wife and I hardly minded having a third parent around to help out where she could. Yet Cici's entry into pseudo-motherhood isn't representative of the experience of all pets. Quite often, the family pet becomes threatened by the disruption of a child, and as a result, a family's new addition can often lead to a subtraction as well.

Yet perhaps the most heartbreaking reason why pet owners say good-bye to their senior pets is because they themselves say good-bye. Though elderly humans and elderly dogs make great companions for one another, the difficult truth is that one must always lead the other into the Great Beyond. And when the human leads, the dog is often left peering back curiously at his limp leash, wondering who—if anyone—will pick up the slack.

Thankfully, places like Bob's House do.

Despite the difficult circumstances that led many of these dogs to Bob's House, as I glance around at the apparent joy shared by these creatures, I tell Amy that if I had four legs, I'd sure hate to leave.

"I think," I half-joke, "that I'd rather stay right here."

"It is nice," Amy admits as a dog brushes against her legs, "but when someone leaves, it opens up room for the next one."

And despite Amy's Herculean efforts to find every dog a home, there's always a next one waiting.

"So give me the spiel," I say. "Why should someone want to adopt a senior dog?"

"Well, if you want to help a homeless dog," Amy begins, "the best way to do it is to take an older dog because they're the most overlooked. We promote them by saying, 'Here's a dog who doesn't require a long walk when you get home from work. He's not going to chew up your stuff. And he's house-trained.' I think that appeals to people. And we know the dogs' temperaments so well," she adds. "People always say, 'Hey, this dog is exactly what you said he would be.'"

Much of Amy's pitch is closely aligned with the arguments set forth by the Senior Dog Project, an advocacy group dedicated to promoting the adoption of older dogs. Their website notes the many benefits of adopting an elderly dog, chief among them the selling point Amy has already made clear—that senior dogs hold few surprises. They're low-maintenance, they transition easily, and most importantly, they rarely possess a wild card. There's never a question of what your dog *might* become; he's already become it.

Most of the changes actually occur on the pet owner's end. Indeed, pet owners reap various rewards for their time spent with animals, though the added time commitment can add to one's stress level as well. In the case of the Quella family, their stress levels have increased exponentially.

Not only has the family endured a financial cost, but they've paid personally as well.

"We're not like other families," Amy admits as she stares down at the dogs sunning themselves at her feet.

"What do you mean?"

"Well, for one, we can't take vacations anymore. We simply don't live a life that allows for it. Now, my husband and I are willing to give that up," she says, "but when you have a fifteen-year-old daughter who has to live in this dysfunctional lifestyle where it's always about the dogs, well, that can be hard on a family."

She explains that the dogs require some level of daily supervision from around 6:00 a.m. until 9:00 or 10:00 at night.

"It's constant," Amy says, shaking her head. "Recently my daughter's school asked us to sign a sheet to allow her to do community service, and I laughed because I thought, 'You live community service! You do it every day!'"

Reaffirming Humane Officer Bekah Weitz's message, Amy is quick to add that while the sacrifices are great, so too are the benefits.

"After a sixty-hour work week," Amy says, "all you have to do is sit down with one of these dogs and suddenly you remember exactly why you do it."

Yet her dogs provide far more than a boost in morale; scientifically speaking, they boost the immune system as well. Recent studies have linked petting a dog with a drop in blood pressure, and owning one has the potential to fortify the heart, lower cholesterol, even help fight depression.

While pet ownership appears to benefit virtually all people in some manner, the population that stands to benefit the most is seniors. As alluded to previously, the pairing of senior humans with senior pets has proved particularly mutually beneficial, so much so that many pet adoption organizations have created "seniors for seniors" programs, which allow senior humans to adopt senior dogs and cats at a reduced rate. Speaking anecdotally, I have often heard of pets offering seniors renewed purpose, reminding them — as Bekah had reminded me — to live one's life with hope.

Yet all anecdotal evidence aside, pets also provide more scientifically measurable benefits for their elderly owners. Over the past few decades, there has been much discussion on the perceived advantages of pairing elderly people with pets, with Sarah Knight and Victoria Edwards's 2008 study, "In the Company of Wolves," offering some of the most persuasive conclusions. According to their study, elderly dog owners gain physical, social, and psychological benefits from their animal companions. Physically, dogs demand regular exercise, and even if their humans neglect their own health, they're unlikely to overlook the health of their dogs. At the prodding of their pups, human companions often find themselves taking several walks a day, a surefire way to keep the blood flowing.

Socially speaking, dogs serve as a social lubricant nearly as effective as alcohol (and without the risk of a hangover). I myself have long reaped the social rewards of dog ownership, trotting Cici around the block frequently enough to allow me to know most of my neighbors by name. These are relationships that have flourished, improving our entire neighborhood one dog at a time.

Finally, there are psychological benefits linked to these dog-inspired physical and social activities. Specifically, physical exercise has proved to serve as a natural antidepressant, and regular socialization with others also wards off feelings of loneliness and depression. In short, it's hard to be alone when you're half of a pack.

Knight and Edwards's study confirms many of the claims found in previous studies, some of which have concluded that pet ownership for the elderly "is associated with significantly less use of health care services." In fact, some research reports a 30 percent decrease in doctor visits for elderly pet owners in comparison to their non-pet-owning counterparts. While this may lead some to believe that pets are the new doctors, let's not go ripping up our insurance cards just yet. Animals don't have all the answers, after all, yet the notion that dogs, cats, and other pets play some scientifically verifiable role in our health serves to further solidify the practicality of our relationship. Though owning a goldfish is unlikely to cure cancer, interacting with one has the potential to increase serotonin and dopamine levels, thereby soothing the human. Which is likely the biological answer for Amy's renewed calm at the end of her sixty-hour work week, a kind of karmic return for her hard work on behalf of her dogs.

Yet Amy—still in the prime of her life—will take her dogs' lessons over their role in her longevity. Though they have taught her many lessons, one always stands out.

"So often we're quick to judge a person by how that person's vehicle looks, or what that person looks like physically," Amy begins. "For instance, initially, I might see a person in one light, but when they come out here and I see how loving they are with the dogs, well, suddenly I'll see that person in an entirely new light. I mean, some of these people would rather give up their own food than their dog's. And so, if dogs have taught me anything," she says slowly, peering around the dog litter box, "it's not to judge a book by its cover. Sometimes the pet you least expect will be your perfect pet. And sometimes the most eccentric people make for the best pet owners."

"What about you?" I ask coyly, squinting into the sun. "Would you consider yourself eccentric?"

"Who, me?" she laughs, a sound soon accompanied by half a dozen howls.

After enduring one final serotonin-releasing slobber bath, I weave through the four-legged frenzy and wave good-bye to both Amy and Nikki.

As I make my way back toward the car, I turn to take one last look at Bob's House.

How odd, I think, shaking my head. *An entire house run by dogs.*

I hardly finish the thought before I'm reminded of the lesson I'd learned within, one I've heard many times before but still manage to forget.

I reach for my notebook, ensuring that I never forget it again.

LESSON #2: DON'T JUDGE A BOOK BY ITS COVER.

THREE

.....

CRUISIN' FOR A BRUISER

It's not the size of the dog in the fight,

it's the size of the fight in the dog.

—MARK TWAIN

Though I've hardly scratched the surface on what our pets stand to teach us, I've already learned one thing for sure: no matter how much we believe our pets to be perfect, there's no such thing as a perfect pet. Yet for the optimistic pet owner, our animals' transgressions merely serve as proof of their individualism.

No, my dog isn't disobedient, an owner might claim, *he's just strong-willed.*

Or: *No, my cat didn't spray on the carpet; she's just expressing herself.* ("Expressing" being the operative word here.)

In truth, I, too, am quick to turn cat piss into lemonade. I want to think the best of my pet, though I admit that my instinct to do so is linked to my fear that my pet's misbehavior might reflect poorly on me. Undoubtedly, a pet's behavior offers some insight on the human-animal relationship, though not nearly as much as can be gleaned by a human's behavior toward a pet.

In the fall of 2011, when a Mennonite family's brood bitch gave birth to a litter of English bulldogs, the family was ecstatic. They'd sold dogs before and were well aware of the high prices that could be garnered for a purebred pup. The litter appeared to be healthy, with the exception of the runt—a smudge-faced whimperer named Bruiser who had trouble standing on his own power. He kicked with his back legs, though his front legs remained splayed at his sides.

Why, the Mennonite family wondered, *wasn't Bruiser developing like the rest of the litter?*

They called upon Tammy Gurklis—a former veterinary technician, as well as the Mennonite family's driver—to take a look at the dog. Tammy agreed, and in December 2011 the pair met face-to-snout for the first time.

When Tammy bent down to examine the brown fur ball, she too soon found herself baffled by the dog's splayed legs. He resembled a miniature, barking bearskin rug, and having never encountered anything quite like him before, all Tammy knew to suggest were regular back massages in the valley between his shoulder blades—a technique she hoped might strengthen the puppy's underdeveloped muscles.

Yet three and a half months later, Bruiser's condition had failed to improve.

Fearing they might never sell the dog, the Mennonite family asked Tammy to take a second look. Tammy agreed, hopeful that if she couldn't fix the problem, she might at least assist in finding the dog a suitable home. Though upon entering Bruiser's urine-soaked, feces-stained, three-by-eight-foot room, it soon became clear that most any home would prove far more suitable than his current situation.

Though Tammy didn't yet know the severity of Bruiser's physical condition—a genetic disease known as bilateral elbow dysplasia—she knew for certain that he'd never recover in his current living quarters.

Desperate to remove him, Tammy sped home, spoke with her husband, Ken, and then called the dog's current owners.

"What's the bottom amount you'll take for the dog?" she asked.

They told her.

"Great," Tammy said. "I'll pick him up Saturday."

Fourteen months later, I pull into Tammy and Ken Gurklis's gravel drive just outside of Thorp, a rural community about an hour east of Eau Claire. The city markets itself as "the gateway to Wisconsin's agricultural epicenter," yet as I drive deeper into the country—passing mile after mile of fields—Thorp begins to feel less like the gateway than the epicenter itself.

Aside from the occasional truck and the telephone poles, I'd seen few signs of life this far out. Though Thorp boasts a population of 1,624, at least 1,622 of its citizens appear to live far closer to town. The pair who remains—Tammy and Ken—awaits my arrival while seated around a circular glass table on the front lawn. Though I've never met them before, I'm so thrilled by signs of civilization that I offer them a frantic wave from my window. I pull the car past a rusting tractor and wagon, then park to the right of their three shuttle vans.

The Gurklises' dogs are the first to greet me. Not Bruiser (whom I soon learn is inside the trailer with his black Lab–springer spaniel friend, Bobbie), but the others—Rufus and his "rat pack," known also as Brutus and Spike. Rufus—an Irish setter–husky mix, and the clear alpha of the group—stretches to the last link of his chain to try to get a good whiff of me. When I lock eyes with him, he stares back with different-colored pupils—one blue, one green. Meanwhile, Brutus and Spike yip from their place just behind him and then, after growing emboldened, begin clawing at the patio's makeshift fence. They're brothers, though they hardly look it, and when I shout a greeting their way, the boxer-terrier mixes respond by springing to the top of their fence, their muzzles peeking just over the edge.

Forty-nine-year-old Tammy stands and makes her way toward me. She's dressed in jean shorts and a pink top, her blonde hair cut just below her shoulders.

"Quite a pack you've got here," I smile.

"Yeah, we like to think so," she agrees. "The eighteen cats are around here somewhere, but they must be hiding."

How, I wonder, *do eighteen cats hide anywhere?*

Ken, Tammy's fifty-six-year-old husband, greets me as well, offering me his leathered hand.

"Good to meetcha," he says, his raspy voice a few octaves lower than the dogs'. A cigarette dangles from his lips, and in his hand is a coffee mug with the words "Hugs and Kisses" stenciled along the front. He's tall, lean, and his good-natured personality seems a perfect fit for his gag T-shirt: an oversized fishing lure beneath the words "Bite Me."

From our place beside the vehicles, Tammy introduces me to Rufus and the rat pack.

"The one barking at you is Rufus," she says. "He's our alarm system. Rufus is what you call a . . ." She pauses. "What do you call him, Ken?"

"A Ford," Ken says, pausing for the punch line. "A found-on-the-road dog."

I smile.

"And then you've got Spike and Brutus," Tammy continues, introducing me to the yippers.

"We'd just lost a dog," Ken explains, "and one day Tammy comes home and says, 'There's a guy whose dog is about to have puppies. We should take a look.' I told her, 'No thanks, I already know what puppies look like . . .'"

Yet judging by the pair of bouncing brothers behind the fence, "taking a look" was only the beginning for Tammy and Ken.

"Now, Brutus is a bit of a scaredy-cat," Tammy admits, nodding to the fawn-colored dog pressing his paws to the fence. "And he's missing a couple of his front teeth because he and Bruiser like to play with the rope . . ."

My ears perk up at the first mention of Bruiser—the primary reason for my pilgrimage. Though I'm excited to meet the Gurklises' menagerie of animals, it was Bruiser—the physically challenged bulldog with the heart of gold—who had initially spurred my visit. I'd learned of his plight thanks to a local newspaper article that detailed his handicap, as well as his efforts to overcome it.

"Tell me about Bruiser," I say, his name hardly leaving my lips before Tammy's face goes aglow as she peers toward the trailer.

"Oh, Bruiser," she sighs, a love-struck smile stuck to her face, "he's our baby . . ."

She recounts her first meeting with her bearskin rug impersonator, then her second—the one that would lead her to adopt him herself.

"When I saw him trapped in that room," Tammy begins, "there was still this bounce about him, this attitude that just screamed, 'Get me out of here!' So we did. We brought him home, started doing therapy on his shoulders, arms, and elbows, and after working with him for two or three months we noticed he was beginning to walk a few inches on his elbows."

"We heard it was good therapy for dogs to swim, but nobody told us that bulldogs *don't* swim," Ken laughs. "We moved a stock tank into the bedroom and everything, and we'd work with him, but as you can imagine, he wasn't much for swimming."

Judging by Bruiser's newspaper photo, I'd pegged him more for an anchor than a buoy.

"Back when he was a puppy," Tammy continues, "we took him to a vet and were told he would never jump on the bed, never climb stairs, never get on top of the couch."

A pause as Ken's straight face turns into a grin.

"The vet lied," he informs me proudly.

The Gurklises' world hasn't been quite the same since Bruiser burst onto the scene. Not only have they shared their bedroom with Bruiser's indoor stock-tank therapy pool, but they've also adjusted their daily schedule to ensure that their golden dog receives no fewer than three full body massages a day.

"Wish I had it that good," Ken jokes.

Despite the veterinarian's pessimistic prognosis, over time, Bruiser's range of motion has seen modest improvements. Months ago, Bruiser could barely place one front paw before the other, but these days, he can climb to the top of an eight-inch-tall step stool, giving him just enough added height to propel himself onto his twin bed—yes, *his* twin bed—situated just a few feet from Tammy and Ken's.

"The rest of the dogs sleep with us on the big bed," Ken says, "plus five, six, seven, eight cats." He shakes his head wearily, then glances toward Tammy. "Some nights you have to fit yourself in like a puzzle piece."

While Bruiser is indeed an integral piece of the family puzzle, Ken doesn't appear overly distraught about not having to share a bed with him. After all, at some point a man must draw the line, though Ken's line, quite generously, extends to a dozen or so animals curled atop his bedsheets.

Despite Bruiser's many gains (in both bed acquisition and range of motion) it's unlikely he will ever gain full control of his front legs as a result of physical therapy alone. It's a reality even Tammy is willing to admit, though this hardly means she's given up on Bruiser's continued improvement.

One day, while accompanying Bruiser to one of his many vet visits, Tammy glanced at a flyer pegged to corkboard. She reached for it, reading with great interest of the newly formed pet orthotics company Forward Custom Design, headquartered out of Eau Claire.

Though she knew little about the burgeoning field of pet orthotics, she was willing to give it a try. After all, if Bruiser would never fully be able to walk on his own power, perhaps an orthotic could be created to assist him.

In April 2012 Tammy called Forward Custom Design and filled the men in on Bruiser's situation.

I'll do anything for him, Tammy explained. *Perhaps you folks can help?*

Traiden Oleson, Terry Kufner, and a coworker—the core of the company—were excited by the challenge. With over sixty combined years of orthotic and prosthetic experience for humans, in 2012 the men decided to apply their expertise to the animal world. By day, they work at Winkley Orthotics and Prosthetics, and after work hours, they share their employer's back room in order to work with pets as well. In their first year of business, they created orthotics for well over thirty dogs, dramatically improving the animals' quality of life.

Upon meeting Bruiser for the first time, Oleson and Kufner took careful note of the bulldog's physical limitations before setting to work on his custom orthotic. They took measurements, made molds, and eventually dreamed up their device—one that now balances before me on the hood of a nearby F-150 pickup in the Gurklises' front lawn.

"It kind of looks like a football player's shoulder pads flipped upside down, with wheels," Tammy says as Ken stands to retrieve it. He walks it over to me, allowing me a closer look from top to bottom: the shoulder molding, the crimson-colored chest padding, the skateboard truck, as well as the three rollerblade wheels attached to the bottom.

"His chest sits here," Ken explains, patting the crimson, "and his front legs go through these holes here. Now, he's real good at pushing," Ken begins, "but . . . he ain't real good at turning."

"What do you mean?"

"Well, when he turns he usually flips," Ken smiles. "I told the guys they should put on some roll bars."

Despite Bruiser's occasional full-throttled roll, Ken agrees he's generally pleased with Forward Custom Design's current model, adding also that the team's already hard at work on an updated version. Rather than adding roll bars, they're experimenting with swapping out the wheels and loosening the truck, thereby keeping Bruiser from resembling an out-of-control stock car racer.

In addition to Bruiser's turning troubles, Tammy and Ken also hope the men of Forward Custom Design might find a way to allow Bruiser to lie down more comfortably while strapped in his brace.

"This lets him sit," Ken agrees, tapping the orthotic, "but Bruiser likes to plop down, and it's kind of hard to do with the wheels holding him up."

Despite these minor adjustments, the Gurklises appreciate their one-of-a-kind orthotic.

"Bruiser just loves it," Tammy confirms. "He really does. We call it the Bruiser Cruiser."

∴

Bruiser is far from the only animal to receive such a chariot. While his front-bodied wheel support is, indeed, rather unique, animal orthotics and prosthetics have been around — in some form — for quite some time. Though the animal-device-production industry has only begun to gain its footing over the last five to ten years, for the past forty years, pet lovers have busily tinkered in garages and workshops to try to help animals make the most of their disabilities. Part James Herriot, part Dr. Frankenstein, it's difficult to pin down a profile for these pet orthotic and prostheses pioneers. Far easier, however, is pinning down their animal recipients.

While household pets still make up the vast majority of animal orthotic and prosthetic users, the media has long been drawn to stories of more exotic animals in need. Such as the story of Winter, the bottlenose dolphin who, in the fall of 2005, became entangled in the rope of a crab trap. After her tail was amputated due to a loss of circulation, the prosthetic and orthotic specialist Kevin Carroll, in conjunction with other experts, designed a silicone and plastic prosthetic, which they affixed to the stub of her tail by way of a gel-like plastic sleeve. The prosthetic was so successful — and the story so inspiring — that in 2011 Warner Brothers released the film version, *Dolphin Tale*. The film raked in over $95 million, making Winter the most famous dolphin since Flipper.

Yet Winter's inspirational story has implications well beyond Hollywood. While animal orthotics and prosthetics have done much to improve the quality of life for animals such as Winter, the human world is seeing payoffs as well. According to journalist Carolyn Sayre, in 2007 an estimated 1.9 million amputees lived in the United States, a figure expected to rise by more than a third by 2020. As Sayre notes, this sudden uptick is primarily the result of the expansion of two populations: those who have lost limbs as a result of diabetes complications and soldiers returning from war. Both benefit from recent improvements in prosthetic and orthotic technologies, improvements that have come as a result of work with a wide range of animals, all of which have served as proverbial guinea pigs. While Kevin Carroll's gel sleeve has done much to improve Winter's quality of life, similar shock-absorbing gels are currently being implemented on human amputees as well, particularly those suffering from painful prosthetics. Carroll's success in easing Winter's pain raised an important question for orthotists and prosthetists everywhere: if it works on a tail, why not an arm or a leg?

Despite the recent successes in the animal-device industry, there remains little agreement on how best to create the most useful and versatile products. The result is a grand array of wheeled carts, plastic feet, and—in the case of Motala, a three-legged, six-thousand-pound Asian elephant—a twenty-two-pound canvas sack stuffed with sawdust. This diversity of design serves as a reminder that we remain in the early phases of the burgeoning of an industry, though as Sayre remarks in her 2007 article for *Time* magazine, we should be reminded also that "attaching a leg to a nimble, bouncing animal like a kangaroo is different from creating a limb for a plodding one like an elephant." In other words, there is no one-size-fits-all model to accommodate every unique circumstance of every unique animal. That prosthetists and orthotists like Oleson and Kufner have dreamed up so many different devices is a testament to their creativity, ingenuity, and commitment to providing animals with disabilities the best lives possible.

Though orthotics such as the Bruiser Cruiser aren't designed to provide services beyond physical support, Tammy remains hopeful that Bruiser's orthotic might offer her dog a boost in his confidence.

As Tammy serves up a dinner of chicken, mashed potatoes, gravy, and coleslaw, she starts in on her speech.

"Imagine if one day something happened that put you in a wheelchair," Tammy says, plopping a helping of potatoes on her plate. "Now, you have strength in your legs, just not enough. So you start in the wheelchair and scoot with your feet. Eventually, you make it to the railings that assist in walking. Maybe the next step is a walker, a cane. Before too long you're walking on your own," she says. "Bruiser's the same way. He's a smart little dog and he picks up on things really quickly."

I'm skeptical.

Can bilateral elbow dysplasia be treated with an orthotic and a boost in confidence?

Sensing my uncertainty, Tammy continues her case.

"Animals are adaptable. Within a week after we brought this home," she says, nodding at the Cruiser, "Ken and I were in the kitchen, and all of the sudden I see Bruiser standing on all fours. He's got his bad paw up, but he's standing using the others. I say, 'Look, look,' trying to get Ken's attention. As soon as he looked, Bruiser went down."

Ken laughs, smiling as he reflects on the scene. "He had this 'Did I do something wrong?' look on his face."

"The point is," Tammy continues, "he's doing that more and more. He's learning how to walk straight, and he's learning how to raise his body."

She pauses to glance at my left hand.

"I noticed you're married," she begins.

I nod, quite curious where this conversation is headed.

"Did you wear a tuxedo?"

"I did."

"Did you wear a cummerbund?"

Did I? I wonder, trying to think back five years to my wedding day.

"No," I admit. "Not me personally. But I know many people do."

"Many do," she agrees. "And we're hoping Bruiser's Cruiser will work much the same way. That it will help do the same work as a corset or a cummerbund—hold his tummy muscles in, which will help him keep his back straight. Help him retrain his muscles."

I nod.

"Even when he's just out here cruising around the yard, we like to give him little challenges."

"Like what?" I ask.

"We'll go places we know he can't go," she explains, "force him to push himself. Sometimes he looks at us like, 'Why won't you help me?' and we have to be like, 'No, we're not going to help you.' It's important he pushes himself to strengthen his back legs."

"Tough love," I agree. "You don't want his crutch to be his crutch."

"Exactly," she says, taking a bite of her chicken. "That's it exactly."

∵

Though bilateral elbow dysplasia is somewhat rare in bulldogs like Bruiser, it — as well as other genetic abnormalities — becomes all the more widespread when genes are passed on in poorly regulated breeding facilities, more commonly known as puppy mills. The American Society for the Prevention of Cruelty to Animals defines puppy mills as "large-scale" breeding facilities "where profit is given priority over the well-being of the dogs." In short, it's the kind of place Tammy Gurklis has no patience for.

Yet quite discouragingly, Americans seems to have plenty of patience for puppy mills. According to the most recent statistics released by the Humane Society of the United States, the United States is home to approximately ten thousand licensed and unlicensed puppy mills, which, taken together, add well over one million puppies to the dog population each year. Given that an estimated three million dogs and cats are euthanized in shelters on a yearly basis, bringing an *additional* million puppies into this fray not only seems counterproductive to our pet overpopulation problems but reaffirms the ASPCA's definition of what a puppy mill is: a place where profits take priority over pets.

As the commercial dog-breeding industry booms, the Animal and Plant Health Inspection Service (APHIS), an agency of the U.S. Department of Agriculture, struggles to enforce federal law. This includes the Animal Welfare Act, which regulates the treatment of animals in "research, exhibition, transport, and by dealers." As enforcement resources run thin — APHIS's budget decreased by $87 million from 2010 to 2012 — profits from puppy mills continue to soar, all while the dogs pay the price. While many in the commercial dog-breeding industry argue that unregulated puppy mills simply bring a bad name to their profession, animal advocates such as People for the Ethical Treatment of Animals (PETA) counter that all commercial dog breeding hurts dogs by contributing to an already glutted market.

Investigations into poorly regulated puppy mills have often revealed conditions so squalid that it seems somewhat remarkable that any of the puppies survive. A few of the more vile practices include the stacking of wire cages—which forces the dogs in the lower cages to endure the excrement dropped by those above—as well as a process known as "de-barking"—the removal of a portion of a dog's vocal chords. In addition to these indignities and abuses, the perpetuation of genetic abnormalities also serves to weaken the breeds. For instance, when a breeder fails to remove a genetically abnormal dog from the breeding pool, the abnormalities have the potential to snowball for generations.

The complexities of dogs' genetic inheritance was recently explored in an episode of PBS's *Nature* entitled "Dogs That Changed the World: Selective Breeding Problems." The episode argues that, much as with human inbreeding, the "selective breeding that created the hundreds of modern dog breeds has put purebred dogs at risk for a large number of health problems." Further, it states that when "genetically similar individuals are intentionally mated," the diseased genes are all the more likely to express themselves in the offspring. "It's like stacking a deck of cards with ten extra aces and ten extra face cards," the episode analogizes; "the loaded deck increases your chance of hitting blackjack in a game of twenty-one—but what you 'win' might be allergies or a predisposition to cancer."

Though I can't speak to the specifics of Bruiser's background, his genetic bingo card undoubtedly saddled him with a disease that—had it not been for the Gurklises—would have lowered his quality of life. Today, Bruiser's quality of life remains high primarily because he stumbled upon a special owner to assist with his special needs. But how many animals fail to find their Tammy and Ken? How many

Bruisers require cruisers, and how many people are willing to pay for them?

∴

At the conclusion of dinner, Tammy excuses herself to the trailer to retrieve her golden dog. I watch anxiously for her return, though when she does, there's no sign of Bruiser.

"Come on, Monkeyhead," she calls from the doorway, "go say hi to B.J."

From my place in the yard, I crane my neck for a better view, though Rufus and his rat pack seemed to have intimidated whatever waits on the other side of the doorway. Moments later, as the other dogs lose interest, Bruiser sees his opportunity and takes it—bursting past a second barrage of barking before Tammy lifts him over the gate and gives him free rein of the yard. The others bark in frustration, though Bruiser ignores them, focusing instead on pushing himself with his rear legs while scuttling forward on his front elbows. His back sinks like the slope of a rollercoaster (giving a whole new meaning to the phrase "downward dog"), but eventually he shudders to a halt just a few feet out of my petting range.

At first, I fail to notice his disability. Sure, I recognize that his gait is a bit peculiar, but in truth, I was expecting him to be far less mobile. Yet the dog before me appears to be moving just fine—not in the most conventional manner, mind you—but moving nonetheless.

"He can walk, don't let him fool you," Ken laughs. "He'll beat us out the door if he wants to go outside."

As if to prove it, Bruiser takes a gigantic leap forward, rubbing his face along the grass as he pushes himself diagonally toward me. But when he gets within three feet or so he stops, bashful, perhaps, or once more playing hard to get.

"Hey, buddy," I say, kneeling and approaching him from the side. "Hey there, boy."

His big dark eyes study me as a slight wheezing releases from somewhere between the folds of his jowls. He's wearing his green-and-blue-plaid collar, but nothing else — his Cruiser momentarily empty on the opposite side of the yard.

"You can say hello, Monkeyhead," Tammy coaxes.

"Come on," Ken encourages, "don't be such a chicken."

I'm not sure if he overcomes being a chicken or simply smells it, but for whatever reason, he begins wriggling forward, allowing me to reach a hand out while he keeps his eyes focused squarely on the chicken on the table.

The sixty-five-pound dog looks as if he's come straight from English bulldog central casting. His brown fur is neatly groomed, his barrel chest protruding like a lumberjack's. He's exactly what I've always envisioned a bulldog to be: thick, stout, and complete with a stubby, corkscrewing tail. Indeed, his movements are different, but he isn't, and within moments, his "normal dog" personality traits reveal themselves as he considers whether to accept the biscuit in my hand.

He scoots forward, sniffs the biscuit between my fingers, and then — after carefully gauging the precise distance between his mouth and the biscuit — devours every last crumb.

"Wow," I say, staring at my newly emptied hand. "That's a pretty good trick."

"Yeah," Tammy agrees, "but do you know what really makes him?"

I shake my head no.

"Well, it's not the fact that he looks like he keeps running into the wall," she laughs. "It's his personality."

"How would you describe his personality?" I ask, taking a bite of chicken as Bruiser — my new best friend — warms my ankles with his breath.

"Bruiser's a curious dog," she begins. "He likes to investigate, but at the same time quick movements scare him. So he's a little leery as well. When people come here and the first thing we hear from them is, 'Aww, look at the poor little puppy! I feel so sorry for him!' we tell them right off the bat, 'Don't feel sorry for him. He doesn't need your pity, he needs your understanding.'"

As does Tammy herself. Though she has long proved herself to be a staunch defender of animals, in the past, Tammy's passion has occasionally caused more trouble than good. Growing up, she'd often "rescue" every last animal on the block, even those not necessarily in need of her assistance. When she was thirteen, she brought home a lost Saint Bernard, only to learn later that it wasn't lost but belonged to her neighbors. Her heart was in the right place, Tammy explains, even if the dog wasn't. On her mother's orders, the Saint Bernard was returned to its rightful owners, but the joy Tammy experienced "rescuing" it would stay with her for years. In fact, it never quite left her.

"You have five dogs and eighteen cats, " I say, repeating her earlier admission. "That's a lot of pets. Some people might call you crazy."

"I have a friend who says people like us are condemned," she admits. "We're condemned because of what we do, because of how we love our animals. But I'll take a hundred instances of being condemned if I can help one animal. I don't take in all of them," she assures me. "I just take the needy ones, the ones people don't want, the ones people think are worthless."

My mind momentarily leaps to Bob's House, to the dogs who were wanted once, but not any longer.

"Now that you've gotten to spend some time with Bruiser," Tammy continues, "do you think he's worthless?"

I shake my head no.

"He's not," she says firmly, staring at his snoring shape beneath the table. "He makes you think about what it means to be a human being."

"What *does* it mean to be human being?" I ask.

She says it's about compassion, about looking out for one another.

To illustrate, she tells me the story of her former cocker spaniel, a beloved pet that was stricken with canine parvovirus.

"I must've spent between $300 to $400 making him well again," Tammy says. "And then one day this woman comes to my yard sale, and she just starts swooning over this dog. She tells me how her family had just recently put their dog down, and that it had been really hard for her son, who had a bad case of asthma. The woman tells me she doesn't know what she's going to do because the loss of this dog was raising new medical issues for her son. So without thinking, I say, 'How about you take this dog? Just give it a good home.'"

Initially, the woman refused, insisting she couldn't possibly afford to pay for it.

"*Take*," Tammy emphasized. "I want you to take this dog. Give it a home. Let it help your child."

The story reveals something I hadn't previously known about Tammy: that when she speaks of compassion, she means compassion for all.

"I'm no hoarder," she says, rubbing a foot against Bruiser's back. "I'm just the type of person who feels bad when an animal's suffering. I can't even stand it when someone kills a daddy longlegs."

Ken leans over to me, whispers, "She even lets mice in the house."

Tammy shoots him a look, her face reddening. "You weren't supposed to tell him that."

"You let mice live in the house?" I laugh. "How do the cats feel about that?"

"Well, they don't love it," she admits. "In fact, they had one trapped once, but I got to him first. I started to bring him outside, but . . . well, it was cold out there," she says, the compassionate animal lover emerging in full force. "And there was this cozy little hole under the trailer where he used to live, so I just let him go right back where he came from."

"Back *inside* the trailer?" I ask, trying to keep from grinning.

"*Under* it," she says, emphasizing the difference. "So technically, not inside."

∵

For the next hour, we discuss everything from *Gilligan's Island* to dog heaven. Through it all, Bruiser appears captivated by our conversation (or at least captivated by the scraps of food left on our plates). But as the sun begins setting over the fields, I steer us back to my central question — the one that led me to Thorp, to Bruiser, and to Tammy and Ken.

"So what does a dog like Bruiser stand to teach us?" I ask.

"A dog like Bruiser," Tammy begins, "well, he teaches me that we all have disabilities. You have a disability, I have a disability, Ken has one. Each of these dogs has one," she says, nodding first to Rufus, then the rat pack, and finally to Bruiser. "Now, what I mean by 'disability' is that there's something you can do that I can't. And there's maybe something I can do that you can't. Bruiser's the same way in his world. There are things he can do that those dogs can't," she says, nodding to Rufus and the others.

She pauses, choosing her words carefully.

"Dogs like Bruiser teach us that you can't believe in can't," she tells me. "You have to be willing to try. Bruiser has more spunk and more spirit and more drive than most dogs, and I think that's what he's taught Ken and me and everyone else who comes to know him. People see this little dog who's working so hard to say, 'Hey, B.J., I'm Bruiser,'" Tammy says, offering her best Bruiser impression. "See me for what I am and not for what I have."

I glance beneath the table and see Bruiser exactly for what he is: a barrel-chested bulldog with a lumberjack build and a pair of people who love him dearly.

"Come on," Tammy says to her dog. "Let's show B.J. what you can do."

Ken stands to retrieve the Cruiser as Tammy riles Bruiser up for his ride.

"Come on, buddy," she calls as Ken leans over, inserting the dog's front paws into the harness. At first Bruiser appears hesitant — *What the heck are you people doing to me?* — though he eventually eases into his familiar ride.

"Come on," Ken urges as he tightens the first of two Velcro straps along Bruiser's back. "We gotta show B.J. how you travel in your buggy."

Bruiser fits neatly into the harness, and after the Velcro is readjusted once more, Tammy loosens the skin folds around his arms. He is no longer a dog, but an astronaut awaiting the countdown, a race-car driver keeping his eyes wide for the green flag.

"Come on, let's show B.J. how you roll," Tammy repeats. "Let's head out to the driveway."

Bruiser seems less sure of this last-minute track change. After all, why would he want to be farther from the chicken scraps?

Demonstrating his ability to put mind over stomach, Bruiser leapfrogs with his back legs, sending his front wheels spinning. He tears into the gravel, kicking up a dust cloud while the other dogs root him on from their place on the porch.

With every push of his paws, Bruiser maintains his stoic grimace. This is serious business, after all, and it becomes all the more serious when chicken scraps enter the equation.

"Look what I got," Tammy sings, dangling a dripping hunk of meat before him.

This time, Bruiser puts stomach over everything (including physics) and finds himself flipped belly-up when his back half fails to keep up with his front.

"Shake it off," Ken calls, "shake it off, boy."

Tammy rights him, slipping him a bit of chicken for his trouble.

His eyes widen as the meat touches his tongue, leading me to wonder if chicken is for Bruiser as spinach is for Popeye. Regardless, it seems to have a similar effect.

Throwing caution to the wind, Bruiser takes one last tear around the yard, showing off the Cruiser's top speeds with seemingly little fear of flipping.

That dog runs himself to exhaustion, and as he pauses to catch his breath, I steal a glance toward Tammy and Ken, both of whom are beaming at their golden boy.

Bruiser wheels toward me as I say my farewells — handshakes for the humans, and a pat behind the ears for their dog.

"I learned a lot today," I say, lifting my eyes from Bruiser to Tammy and Ken. "Thank you all."

The Gurklises wave as I slip into my own wheels, start the engine, and begin backing out of the drive. In the rearview, I spot Bruiser standing tall in his Cruiser, watching curiously as I manage to turn the car without even flipping it. He doesn't offer any indication that I've impressed him with my driving skills, though he's certainly impressed me with his.

As I head west toward Eau Claire, I reflect on Bruiser's lesson, one that reminds me that though none of us are perfect, we're all perfectly suited to improve. It's a lesson Tammy and Ken have observed throughout Bruiser's life, one that their chicken-loving dog demonstrates daily. I glance down into my open notebook and see my scrawl staring back at me:

LESSON #3: DON'T BELIEVE IN CAN'T.

FOUR

·····

FOLLOW THE LEADER

The dog must have perfect obedience and yet he cannot be a machine; he must have certain initiative to take care of situations as they come up. He must obey all commands and yet be ready to take matters into his own realm.

—DOROTHY EUSTIS, "THE SEEING EYE,"

SATURDAY EVENING POST, NOVEMBER 5, 1927

I park my bike in the nearest rack and make my way toward the house. It's another perfect summer morning—blue sky with cotton candy clouds—and as I walk toward McKinley Street in my home of Eau Claire, I see that I'm not alone in enjoying the beautiful day. A pair of dogs frolic in a nearby yard, zooming past one another, backs arched, engaged in serious play.

They spot me—bark—though I have to pass on their invitation to join the fun.

"Not today," I say, "sorry, guys. I've got a prior engagement."

What I don't tell them is that the engagement is with another dog—a service animal named Luna—along with her human, Dr. Katherine Schneider.

Prior to leaving my own home, I'd been careful to scribble Kathie's address onto my palm, though following my bike ride across town, the address has turned mostly to smudge. I've narrowed it down to two houses, when I notice a small sticker in the nearest home's front-door window, offering me a clue:

In case of emergency, please see mailbox for information on assistance dog.

Confident I've found the right place, I knock three times on the door.

Kathie's quaint, blue, one-story home stands just a few hundred feet from our shared university campus, where she served as a clinical psychologist for fourteen years. Yet for Kathie, the choice of a blue home was not nearly as important as its proximity to work—a distance easily covered by her and her Seeing Eye dog, even on the coldest, snowiest Wisconsin days.

Born in Kalamazoo, Michigan, in 1949, Kathie spent the early years of her childhood wholly unaware of her blindness. In fact, it wasn't until the summer of 1952—when three-year-old Kathie and her older brother were tasked with pulling dandelions at a penny per head—that she began to notice a discrepancy in her and her brother's output. While Kathie's eyesight forced her to search tirelessly for each dandelion, her brother snatched them up by the fistful.

In her book *To the Left of Inspiration: Adventures in Living with Disabilities*, Kathie describes the frustration she felt during one such summer reaping, how her brother's pile of dandelions grew and grew while her own stayed mostly stagnant.

At just three years of age, Kathie had already learned a lesson that would long stay with her: sometimes, for no good reason, life simply isn't fair. It was a lesson echoed back to her throughout her career as a psychologist, and one that she helped more than a few college-aged students come to grips with as they walked through her office door.

And it was a lesson I, too, had learned, most recently as a result of my time spent with Bekah Weitz, Amy Quella, and the Gurklises, as well as the animals entrusted into their care. Life wasn't fair for the pup Bekah found tethered to the tree beneath the burning sun, or for Amy's abandoned senior dogs, or for Tammy and Ken's beloved

Bruiser. As all of these people and pets have proved, life's unfairness takes many forms, and no one—human or animal—is ever wholly protected.

Though Kathie first learned of the world's unfairness on that summer morning in 1952, she was reminded of it again in her early forties when, in addition to her blindness, she was diagnosed with fibromyalgia.

"Wasn't one disability my fair share?" Kathie asks in her book. "Why two?"

Though I prefer to think otherwise, I suspect the universe cares little for doling out disabilities—or anything—in "fair shares." While I, like Kathie, have often called upon the universe to answer for its cosmic imbalances, I've yet to receive a reply. Which leads me to wonder if the universe simply refuses to answer to fair shares, or to the cosmos, or even karma. Perhaps when it ignores our pleas with equanimity, we learn a greater truth: despite there being little rhyme or reason for the hand we've been dealt, our only choice is to play it. And play it we do, if for no other reason than the hope that we might receive a better hand next time around. Though keep this in mind also: even if our cards don't change, the game might, and thus what was once a weakness might become our strength.

I think back to Tammy's remarks on one of the many lessons Bruiser taught her: how each us of is afflicted with a disability—some of which are simply more apparent than others. Keeping with the playing card metaphor, it's apparent that some of us keep our cards close to our vest, while others lay them on the table for all to see. Yet what's less apparent is that oftentimes we don't have a choice in the matter. For instance, while an outsider likely can't visually observe Kathie's fibromyalgia, her blindness is more evident.

Today I am the outsider, and a bit nervous, as I wipe my sweaty palms on my shorts and wait for Kathie to answer the door. After today, I hope I'll no longer resort to extended metaphors when trying to describe the lives of people with disabilities. Rather, I hope I'll begin to see my own imperfections with a bit more clarity.

I hear Kathie fiddling with the lock and then the squeak of a door swinging wide.

"Well, hi there," Kathie smiles, and then, without missing a beat: "This is Luna."

I've hardly shaken Kathie's hand before I bend to shake Luna's as well.

The two-year-old yellow Labrador greets me as most dogs do — by pumping her nose directly into my crotch. It's a greeting I've come to expect from dogs of a certain height (and one reason why my calf-high Cici seemed a good choice when we adopted her).

"Hey there, girl," I say, trying to redirect her head. "What a friendly dog you are."

"Come on in," Kathie welcomes me. "Help yourself to a magazine."

I get the joke as soon as I glance into Kathie's living room, where I observe several towering stacks of *Harper's* and the *New York Times Book Review*, among other periodicals, all of them sheathed in braille covers.

"You're quite the voracious reader," I say.

"Oh," she shrugs, "I try to keep up."

It's the first time I've been inside a blind person's home, and within moments, most of my assumptions are dismantled. As we walk toward the table, we pass several landscape paintings lining the walls, which debunks my first myth, that a blind person likely has little interest in visual art. As we walk farther we pass a color TV complete with VCR, which debunks my second myth, that blind people have little use for these items, either.

Within moments it's clear that I am the blind one, embarrassingly ignorant about a way of life different from my own.

The paintings, I realize, *are for me. And don't I, too, enjoy listening to the television?*

"What are you drinking?" Kathie asks, interrupting my thoughts.

I spot the three boxes of tea on the dining room table and say tea will be just fine.

"Tea it is," she agrees, walking toward the kitchen while Luna keeps me company in the living room. As Kathie readies the water, I wonder why Luna—the highly trained Seeing Eye dog—has opted to socialize with me rather than perform her guide work. Sensing my confusion, Kathie explains that Luna is currently off-duty, and thus her socializing is acceptable behavior.

"In the house," Kathie says, placing my mug in the microwave, "her main job is just being a dog."

"She seems to have it down," I say as Luna's nose thumps my hand, demanding a pet.

Peering back into the living room, I spot bookshelves and tables overflowing with animal figurines. They're mostly dogs, but plenty of birds, too—a menagerie of crows and parrots, among various other flocks. On the floor is a pack of dog statues, accompanied by a few more canines painted on signs and scattered throughout. As I scan the living room a bit closer, I begin to realize that almost every object in the room is an homage to animals, another clue that helps me understand the depth of Kathie's connection with her four-legged partner.

The microwave dings and Kathie hands me my steaming-hot cup of water.

"Help yourself to whatever kind you like," Kathie says, nodding to her tea selection as we take our seats across from one another at the table. Luna lays belly-up between us, anxiously awaiting a scratch.

Unaware of Luna's request, the gray-haired, sixty-four-year-old Kathie folds her hands on the table in preparation for our interview. As I double-check my notes, I glance up to notice Kathie's dog-covered SPCA T-shirt, bringing the animal paraphernalia count even higher.

"You know, originally, I was allergic to dogs," Kathie tells me, taking a sip of her tea.

"Really?" I ask, shooting a glance toward Luna. "How'd you work that out?"

Kathie regales me with the tale. How at twenty-four, as she completed her graduate work at Purdue University, she realized that due to the competitiveness of academic careers, a job offer might very well lead her to a big city, in which case a guide dog might come in handy. The prospect of navigating New York or Chicago or any other metropolis by cane alone seemed a daunting proposition, and one Kathie hoped to avoid. And so she placed herself on the receiving end of a series of desensitization shots, hopeful the inoculations might lessen her allergies. Remarkably, the shots worked.

"I used a long cane before that," Kathie explains, and though she'd grown proficient with it, when she was paired with her first dog, Cindy, in 1973, she soon learned of the many advantages a dog has over a cane.

"Like what?" I ask.

"Oh, just simple stuff," Kathie says. "Like when you're in a Wisconsin winter and there's fresh snowfall that hasn't been shoveled. With a cane, you're out there poking around for where the path is, but with a dog—if they know where they're going—they'll drag you right on through."

I smile at the thought of Cici serving as a miniature snowplow and dragging me through the drifts.

"The image is a lot different, too," Kathie continues. "With a cane there's kind of a bubble around people with disabilities, and people don't break through nearly enough. Whereas if you've got a dog, first the kids come, then the parents come to get the kids, and pretty soon you've got a crowd. Sometimes it's a pain in the anatomy," she smiles, "but most of the time it's really good."

For over forty years, Kathie and her nine Seeing Eye dogs have busily burst this bubble, offering a welcoming hand (and paw) to those who might've otherwise shied away.

"I hope to make the fifty-year club," Kathie remarks. "If you work with guide dogs for fifty years, they give you a little dog statue."

"Who gives you the statue?" I ask.

"The school," she says simply.

She's referring to the Seeing Eye, the nation's oldest guide dog training facility, located in Morristown, New Jersey, about a forty-mile drive west of Manhattan. Kathie informs me that not just any old guide dog can be deemed a "Seeing Eye" dog. To earn the prestigious title, a dog must first complete its training at the Morristown facility.

While America didn't invent the concept of the guide animal, over the past eighty year, a significant portion of the United States' blind population has embraced the idea. Today an estimated ten thousand guide dog teams are at work in the United States alone. However, the history of guide dogs traces back to Germany, notes writer Mark Ostermeier, when in the midst of World War I a German doctor named Gerhard Stalling observed his German shepherd assisting a blind veteran. The dog's unprompted service piqued Stalling's interest, causing the curious doctor to wonder what a dog might be capable of if specially trained to assist blind soldiers. World War I's introduction of chemical warfare unleashed a new breed of destruction into the world, and though the proverbial "dogs of war" hadn't changed, Stalling began hypothesizing how actual dogs might be more effectively utilized in wartime. Since German doctors had struggled to return their eye-injured soldiers to full sight, Stalling considered another tack: improving the soldiers' quality of life by pairing them with highly trained canines.

In 1916 Stalling founded the world's first guide dog school in Oldenburg, Germany, with at least twelve additional branches to open within the next decade. In total, these facilities churned out over four thousand specially trained dogs, forever altering Germany's blind community.

Meanwhile, across the sea in America, Dorothy Eustis had also become keenly interested in the rare combination of intelligence and docility she'd observed in her German shepherd, Hans von Saarbrücken. For over a decade Eustis had marveled at Hans's skill set, leading her to wonder, as Stalling had, what a properly trained dog might do.

In the 1920s she and her second husband, George Eustis, moved to their estate — Fortunate Fields — in Vevey, Switzerland, where they set to work transforming their home into an experimental training facility dedicated to producing highly trained dogs. Prior to his death in 1915, Eustis's first husband, New York state senator Walter Abbott Wood, had worked closely with his wife in selectively breeding dairy cows in order to increase milk production. Dorothy Eustis hoped to apply the same selective breeding philosophy to dogs.

Together, the Eustises scouted desirable dogs throughout Switzerland and Germany, believing that only with the proper combination of training and breeding could a dog reach its full potential. Their search paid off, and within three years' time, they had acquired dogs so carefully bred and rigorously trained that the Eustises were soon approached by the Swiss state police, the Swiss army, and the Red Cross, all of which recognized the value of the dogs and wanted a few of their own.

While the Eustises excelled in their elite dog training business, during a trip to Potsdam, George Eustis's eyes were opened to yet another possibility for their pups — one that he knew would be of great interest to his wife. After observing the success of Potsdam's local guide dog school, he called upon Dorothy to observe the dogs firsthand. Though her expectations were initially quite low, she soon found herself pleasantly surprised by the work being done in Potsdam. So impressed, in fact, that Eustis felt compelled to write about Potsdam's success in the November 5, 1927, issue of the *Saturday Evening Post*, an article that served as America's introduction to guide dogs.

As Eustis smartly pointed out in her article, the dogs in the Potsdam school provided not only mobility assistance for their blind humans, but something less tangible as well.

"I shall never forget the change that came over one man," Eustis recounted. "It was as though a complete transformation had taken place before my eyes. One moment it was an uncertain, shuffling blind man, tapping with a cane, the next it was an assured person, with his dog firmly in hand and his head up, who walked toward us quickly and firmly, giving his orders in a low confident voice."

The article sparked the interest of America's blind community, and in particular, the interest of a twenty-year-old insurance salesman named Morris Frank. After reading Eustis's article, Frank became convinced that a dog such as those trained in Potsdam could dramatically assist him in overcoming the obstacles he'd faced since becoming stricken with blindness four years prior. He wrote to the Eustises, traveled from Nashville to Vevey, and after five weeks of intensive training at Fortunate Fields, returned to America fully committed to popularizing guide dogs throughout the country. Accompanied by his own recently acquired guide dog—a female German shepherd named Buddy—he began a grand tour, a public relations campaign aimed at persuading America of the value of guide dogs, at least enough to warrant opening a guide dog school stateside.

In 1929 Frank's dream came to fruition. While the rest of the country sank into the grips of the Great Depression, Dorothy Eustis and Morris Frank's unwavering commitment to bringing guide dogs to America prompted them to cofound the Seeing Eye in Nashville. By 1931 the school had moved to Morristown, where it continues to pair hundreds of blind people with dogs every year.

However, as Kathie can attest, the process of acquiring a Seeing Eye dog is neither easy nor cheap. According to the organization's website, a potential Seeing Eye dog's life begins at the school's breeding station, where—true to the Eustises' vision—a highly selective breeding process ensures the dogs are born genetically geared for their task. The puppy is raised at the school for seven weeks, then sent to a volunteer foster family for the next sixteen months, where the puppy is socialized and taught basic obedience skills. At eighteen months of age the dog begins training at the Seeing Eye. If successful, the dog is then matched with a human, at which point the human travels to Morristown for three to four weeks of intensive training alongside the dog.

It's a journey Kathie has taken on nine separate occasions, one that always proves bittersweet. After all, if a human travels to Morristown it's most likely because his or her previous Seeing Eye dog has either retired or passed on, thereby warranting a replacement. But as Kathie knows all too well, a dog can never be replaced, even if the dog's skills can be. Though Kathie has steeled herself for this solo plane trip several times before, she admits the journey never gets easier, practically speaking. For a blind person, travel is difficult even with a guide animal (ever see an airport restroom for an animal?), and the trip becomes all the more challenging without one.

Upon arriving at the Seeing Eye, the human half of the human-dog team often faces emotional challenges as well. While Kathie enjoys meeting her new dogs, there is always some reluctance in doing so. The old dog, like an old friend, is as comfortable as an old pair of shoes. A new dog, much like new shoes, requires some breaking in.

"Part of the art of matching dogs and owners is to match potentials," Kathie explains in her book. "To predict how an adolescent dog will mature, and what that blind person's needs will be in several years, is an art indeed." Though pairing a Seeing Eye dog with a human doesn't require a Chuck Woolery–style "Love Connection," personalities and potentials must indeed sync, and sometimes they don't — at least not at first.

Kathie shares with me the story of an opera singer who was paired with a German shepherd. At first they got along just fine, the German shepherd performing his duties admirably. Yet every time the singer took the stage, her solos always became howling duets.

"Needless to say, that pairing didn't work out," Kathie smiles.

In 1973, on her first day at the Seeing Eye, Kathie, too, became abruptly aware of the difficulties of finding the perfect match. Under the watchful eye of a military-officer-turned-dog-trainer, Kathie and her first dog, Cindy, began feeling one another out.

"So we're out walking the street and Cindy is about two feet from me," Kathie recounts. "She knows what to do, but she has no reason to do it for me. Yet. So we're out walking when suddenly she slams me into a tree and then looks back at the trainer like, 'Hey, did I get rid of her?' That was kind of our introduction," Kathie laughs, "and I thought to myself, 'Do I really want to be doing this?'

"I had the same stereotype I think a lot of people have," Kathie continues, "which is that Seeing Eye dogs are perfect, that they're robots or something. But they're not. They have their own feelings, personalities, and you have to take all of that into account. I remember one time the trainer said, 'If you and the dog both have to go to the bathroom, go take care of the dog first.' That has stayed with me all these years. It was good advice about priorities. Always put your dog first."

Though my interactions with Luna are limited, already I'm getting the sense that she's embraced the opposite advice, putting her person first instead. Which is, of course, the beauty of their arrangement, one in which Kathie continually makes Luna her top priority, while Luna does the same for Kathie.

If only human relationships could manage such a selfless arrangement, I think.

Despite her near-perfect behavior, judging by her introductory crotch sniff, Luna has proved herself to be a creature of free will as well, an invaluable trait for a guide dog. While in most instances guide dogs are meant to serve as loyal foot soldiers, on occasion they must know to break ranks, disrupt the hierarchy, and tell their humans no.

"The big differences between a pet dog and a guide dog is something called intelligent disobedience," Kathie explains. "Basically, it means that if I tell Luna to move forward into a street and it isn't safe she has to disobey. However," Kathie laughs, careful not to give Luna too much credit, "learning when she's disobeying *intelligently* and when she's just disobeying when she sees a hamburger wrapper on the ground, well, that takes at least six months to figure out."

"My dog, Cici, disobeys all the time," I agree, "but never intelligently."

Adding another wrinkle to the relationship are the instances in which the human must overrule the dog that has already attempted to overrule the human. For instance, if a blind person knows the way down a staircase, then that person will issue a command informing the guide dog of this information. Then the guide dog will stand down, momentarily halting its usual precautionary measures. I can only imagine the anxiety this must cause the dogs, all of whom are left trying to understand the rationale behind complicating the simplicity of their follow-the-leader approach. But as the human half of a guide dog team will tell you, there are always two ends of a harness — two brains involved — though only one can lead at a time.

I ask Kathie to tell me a bit more about how a dog learns to lead — specifically, how a Seeing Eye dog learns to interact in a new environment.

"When I first get a new dog, I teach them the words 'in' and 'out' and 'up' and 'down' so I can go into an unfamiliar building and say 'up' and they'll find the stairs," Kathie explains. "But I've noticed something in several of my dogs. When they get to be middle-aged — about seven or so — instead of showing me the stairs, they'll show me the elevator. They decide there's an easier way to do 'up.'"

"Sounds like your dogs really do have a mind of their own," I say.

"They do," Kathie agrees without hesitation. "And I give them the space *to* have a mind of their own."

And for good reason.

Kathie shares the story of a walk she and her dog once took with a "directionally challenged" sighted friend.

"I had my dog, my sighted friend, and my GPS," Kathie explains. "And we were on a corner downtown, trying to figure out how to get home. The dog was thinking one thing, my directionally challenged friend was thinking another, and the GPS was off thinking something else. I thought to myself, 'I got too many votes here . . .'"

"So what'd you do?" I ask. "Who'd you go with?"

"I went with the dog," Kathie shrugs, as if the answer was obvious, "and the dog was right."

∵

Though most pet owners know all too well the heartache of saying good-bye to a beloved animal, far fewer grasp the grief a human feels when saying good-bye to a guide animal. After all, how can a person ever repay a creature that has dedicated her entire life to service? Despite Kathie's training as a psychologist, she offers little advice to help assuage the pain felt by those who lose their guide dogs, or, for that matter, assistance animals of any species.

While guide dogs remain the most popular species of assistance animal, various other species have recently joined their ranks, from miniature horses to monkeys on down. As writer Rebecca Skloot makes clear in a 2008 *New York Times* article, each species possesses its own unique skill set, offering people with disabilities a wider selection of animal partners. Miniature horses, for instance, are "mild-mannered, trainable, and less threatening than large dogs," Skloot contends, not to mention their 360-degree range of vision and their thirty-year lifespan. For many people with disabilities, the miniature horse's longevity is the species' greatest benefit, particularly when compared to the abbreviated life of a guide dog. The extended working relationship shared between people and miniature horses not only ensures fewer substitutions on the team but, perhaps of equal importance, spares the human from having to say good-bye any more than necessary.

"Every good-bye is hard," Kathie admits, a slight waver developing in her throat as she recalls the eight dogs that came before Luna. "And it's especially hard because there are three parts to the good-bye."

In my observations as a pet owner, the final good-bye to a pet has always seemed a two-step process: determining the pet's low quality of life and then taking responsible means to end the suffering. Throughout my adult life, I've been fortunate to never have to take either step alone. Nevertheless, I've watched my parents tread this trail on multiple occasions. For them, the decision to drive the animal to the vet was never easy, though they recognized the necessity of their task. But as Kathie explains to me, saying good-bye to a guide dog is different and requires one additional step.

"Three parts," she repeats. "There's the decision making, there's the actual moment when you take them to their new place, and then there's the eventual good-bye to death. And though they're not in service to me at that point, I've been at most of the final passings."

"The first step is deciding to *retire* a dog," I say, beginning to understand the guide dog's unique good-bye.

Kathie nods. "And when it's a retirement decision, I don't pull any punches with them. I talk about it with them, tell them, 'I wish this wasn't happening, but I pledge to you that I will find a good place for you to be where you will be loved and needed.'"

"When does the average guide dog retire?" I ask.

"Usually somewhere between the ages of eight and ten."

"And then you find the dog a new home?"

"I do," Kathie nods. "I interview a lot of people and I make sure I stay true to my pledge. But the actual taking of the dog . . . that's a real tough piece for me. Packing the bag, writing up a summary of likes and dislikes, the things they need to know."

Despite her efforts to maintain her composure, when leaving a newly retired dog in the hands of a new owner (the guide dog's second good-bye), Kathie admits she barely ever makes it out the door before breaking down.

"When I go to drop off a dog, I always bring a friend I trust to see me being a basket case. I'll walk in, I'll visit, I'll drop off the supplies, drop off the dog, and then my friend gets to lead me out of there and I say, 'Good-bye, be good,'" Kathie says, imitating the cheery trill she fakes for the dog's benefit. "But as soon as I get outside and the door is shut, I dissolve."

As she explains the procedure, I fear she may dissolve once more right here in her living room, but instead, she reaches for Luna, offering her dog a scratch that calms them both.

"When I walk out the door, they don't follow me," she says. "I don't think it's because they're saying, 'Hallelujah, I don't have to work anymore.' I think they've just gotten to that point in their minds when they know this is how it's going to be."

"They've got a mind of their own," I say, echoing Kathie's earlier remark, "and that sounds like a good thing."

"Mostly," Kathie agrees.

Though Kathie's nine Seeing Eye dogs have taught her an

incalculable number of lessons, the lesson she remembers most she learned from her first dog, Cindy, whose independent streak left an indelible mark on Kathie.

"She's the one who taught me to be positive," Kathie explains.

Kathie takes me back to a sweltering-hot Arkansas day many years back when she and Cindy began their trek across a field on their way to work.

"It was about 90 percent humidity, as it often is in Arkansas," Kathie begins, "and Cindy was walking slower and slower, and it was getting hotter and hotter, and I was crabbing at her. 'Hurry up. Let's go and get to our building and into the air conditioning.' So she starts going slower and slower and I'm crabbing louder and louder, and finally, once we're in the middle of the field, she just sits down on her big Labrador rump and that was it."

Suddenly at the mercy of the dog, Kathie realized she'd have to try something different.

"So I started to sweet talk her," Kathie remembers. "'Oh, Cindy, you're hot. Oh, Cindy, I know just how you feel.' When I talked to her, she sort of cocked her head like, 'Hmm, something's changing here . . .' So I said, 'Come on, we can do this,' and sure enough, she got up and we got moving. Of course, I didn't mean a word of it," Kathie continues. "Truthfully, I wanted to kill her, but I learned that being positive was useful."

It was a lesson she soon integrated into the human world as well.

"Eventually I thought to myself, 'Well, it works on animals, it might work on people, and if it works on people, it might just work on you. Maybe you could look for what's right in yourself instead of just what's wrong.' So that's what I did, and it was a life changer," Kathie concludes. "And I didn't learn that from any psychology class I ever took. I learned that from a dog."

I reach my hand down to Luna, offering a final pat.

"They teach us a lot, don't they?" I ask.

"They sure do," Kathie agrees.

Kathie and Luna escort me to the door, and after we say our

good-byes, I'm left alone to gather my thoughts beneath the summer sun. Within seconds, I'm interrupted by the barks of the neighbor dogs, still engaged in their serious play.

"Good dogs," I say as I pass them. "What very good dogs you are."

They don't understand a word I say, but it still feels good to practice what I've learned.

I reach for my pen, then flip wide the notebook.

LESSON #4: BE POSITIVE.

FIVE

.....

I LEFT MY HEART IN HARTSDALE

The best place to bury a dog is in your heart.

—FROM A LETTER FOUND AT HARTSDALE PET CEMETERY

In the spring of 1992 our Doberman, Sandy, began to grow weak. It started in the hips, followed by a buckling in the knees, until finally, after months of my parents carrying her back and forth from her beanbag chair to the lawn, they informed me it was time to say good-bye to Sandy for good.

Why? I wondered. *Was she going on a trip?*

I was in the first grade and, until that day, had been wondrously naïve to the ways of Death. And so, when my parents informed me that Sandy would not be waiting for me when I returned home from school, I assumed she simply had other plans.

Chasing squirrels, I figured, *or the mail carrier.*

As it turned out, my parents were the ones with the plan.

"Come on, B.J.," they coaxed, "say good-bye now."

I did, oblivious to the finality of this particular good-bye.

Quite casually, I offered my beloved first dog one final pet, one last nuzzle, and then, at the sound of the bus honk, left her there forever. The last Sandy ever heard of me was the whine of the screen door slamming shut.

When I returned home from school eight hours later, Sandy's

beanbag chair sat empty. Likewise, her collar—now with no neck to fill it—lay sprawled like a snake on the table. I had a hard time understanding just how "gone" she was until days later, when I was shown her ashes zipped into a plastic bag and placed in a copper tin.

Upon viewing her ashes for the first time, my seven-year-old mind dismissed the more existential questions and instead focused on the practicalities.

Such as: where does one bury a dog?

The backyard seemed the most logical choice, but then I began wondering what might happen if we moved. Would we be forced to exhume her, or would we simply leave our old girl behind?

We did move, just a few years later, but since we'd never gotten around to burying Sandy, she just came with us. We taped her tin into a cardboard box and drove her to our new home across town. There, she would be destined to sit on a backroom bookshelf for years, her tin untouched and forgotten. It was, for a time, precisely how we wanted to say good-bye to her: by not saying good-bye at all.

Over the years, our family would lose many pets, though only Sandy's ashes remained on that backroom bookshelf. Once our family laid down roots, the other pets received more proper burials. My father—a gravedigger himself—understood that the best place to bury a dog is any place the ground is soft, which, for us, meant the shady glen in the woods at the edge of our property. There, beneath the bramble and trees, my father dug hole after hole, employing pieces of broken brick as markers.

If asked why we failed to bury Sandy, I could offer any number of excuses, though none would pass the litmus test of truth. Due to strictly enforced ordinances, city dwellers have long struggled to bury their pets, though this was hardly an issue for us in Fort Wayne, Indiana. Our delay in burial couldn't be blamed on bureaucracy, though for over a hundred years, grieving pet owners from larger cities often pointed fingers in that direction. As many learned, while losing a pet was traumatic, so too was the indignity of having no place to bury the body.

This was the case in 1896, when a distraught woman burst into New York veterinarian Dr. Samuel Johnson's office and pleaded for help. Her beloved dog had died and a city ordinance precluded her from burying the body anywhere within city limits.

Can you help? she begged. *Is there anything you can do?*

The forty-two-year-old veterinarian attempted to calm the woman, assuring her they'd find a solution. After a bit of thought, Johnson considered a few acres of apple orchards he owned in the nearby hamlet of Hartsdale, about twenty miles north of Manhattan.

Perhaps, Johnson offered, *you might find a suitable spot for your dog beneath the trees?*

And so began the first of many pilgrimages to what would soon become Hartsdale Canine Cemetery (later renamed Hartsdale Pet Cemetery) — "the oldest continuously operated commercial burial ground for animals in the Western world," according to Mary Thurston, the cemetery's official historian and the author of *The Lost History of the Canine Race.*

In a recent phone interview, Thurston explained how the formation of Hartsdale at the end of the nineteenth century contributed to an already-in-progress watershed moment in America's human-pet relations.

"People were moving away from their families and into the cities for the first time," Thurston told me, "and oftentimes pets were the only things these people came home to. And so I think it was inevitable that people were going to get more attached to their animals than they ever had back on the farm, where dogs typically stayed in the barn. Now the dog was no longer in the barn, but on the couch, or on the bed in the apartment."

Simply put, the urbanization of America altered not only skylines but the proximity between people and their pets. Suddenly pet owners had a front-row seat on the emotional lives of their animals and, upon their animals' deaths, often became a bit emotional themselves.

"Here's this booming city," Thurston explained, "and people are getting attached to their animals like never before. But when these pets died, there was nowhere to bury them in the city. People were told to put their pets out on the curb with the garbage."

It was a solution that didn't sit well with the new breed of pet owner, particularly in New York City. Finding themselves with no alternative, pet owners took to Central Park under cover of darkness, their shovels glinting off lantern lights.

"If I had to guess," Thurston joked, "I'd say Central Park is probably the biggest pet cemetery in the world."

Perhaps in an attempt to minimize unsanctioned grave digging in one of America's most well-known parks, to this day, the New York City Department of Sanitation still offers local residents free curbside pickup of dead pets. But they will do so only if the pet owner complies with protocol, which means placing one's departed pet in a plastic bag, along with a taped note that reads, "Deceased animal inside."

Yet for many, the idea of disposing of one's pet in the same manner we dispose of our garbage seems an unfitting tribute to the animal. As such, many pet owners prefer cremation, where an animal can live a long afterlife on a backroom bookshelf, or on a mantle, or spread any number of places throughout the world.

But there is a smaller population of pet owners who take another approach: interring their animals in pet cemeteries such as Hartsdale, where men like Ed Martin Jr. ensure that the memory of the dead keeps on living.

∵

Seventy-two-year-old Ed Martin Jr. — Hartsdale's current president and director — has dedicated much of his life to America's animals. Whereas vets are tasked with preserving our pets' lives, Martin assists pet owners in preserving their legacies.

Had my family been more fully informed of pet cemeteries in 1992, perhaps we would have gotten around to burying Sandy. At the very least, a pet cemetery would've provided more solemnity than a backroom bookshelf, and perhaps, a little more closure. Keep in mind, however, that in 1992, most of what Americans knew of pet cemeteries they'd learned from Stephen King, whose horror novel *Pet Sematary* offered a less-than-ideal portrait of the final resting place of pets. Despite the book's negative cultural impact on pet cemeteries, Hartsdale continues to thrive, as it has for most of the last century. Ed Martin Jr. deserves much of the credit. He, along with his predecessors—Chris Scheu and George Lassen—took the helm of Hartsdale throughout the cemetery's transitional periods. Following Dr. Johnson's death in 1937, the Johnson children—to whom Johnson left his estate—were at a loss as to how best to continue what their father had started. They didn't want their father's pet cemetery to fall into disarray, but they also didn't want to be responsible for its continual upkeep. Adding to this was the financial blow that struck the cemetery throughout the Depression. Despite Americans' growing love for their pets, heartstrings and purse strings didn't align. Thus, much of America's cash-strapped populace put a hold on all nonessentials, including pet burials. From 1937 until 1941, the Johnson children sought out a dual solution. What the cemetery needed, they reasoned, was a few dedicated people who were up to the challenge.

Enter Chris Scheu and George Lassen, two men whose garage business happened to be in its own financial straits. Scheu—a longtime neighbor to the cemetery—had offhandedly mentioned his interest in Hartsdale to a caretaker, and as a result, soon found himself seated around the negotiating table to buy a business he knew virtually nothing about. Lassen was brought on board as well, and though the men hardly had the capital to purchase the cemetery, according to Martin, the Johnson children were more interested in ensuring the cemetery's continuation than in profiting from the sale.

Scheu and Lassen purchased Hartsdale in 1941, committing themselves to the goal of restoring the cemetery to its former grandeur. Yet doing so was no easy task. The previous twenty-five years had taken a toll on Dr. Johnson's once-idyllic orchard, and with little money left over to invest in upkeep, it soon became evident to the new owners that Hartsdale was in need of an updated business model.

Though the cemetery was born of humble roots, as the years wore on, more extravagant pet memorials began popping up between the wood-shingle markers of the past—a juxtaposition that served as visual proof of an evolving clientele. Initially, burial sites were priced between fifteen and twenty-five dollars for dogs and slightly less for cats, though as Dr. Johnson discovered, many pet owners were prepared to pay much more.

Chief among them was Mrs. M. F. Walsh, who in 1915 not only purchased several plots but reportedly paid an additional $25,000 for the construction of a granite mausoleum to house her dead pets, a sum that equates to around half a million dollars in today's money.

Walsh wasn't alone in her elaborate send-off, and in an effort to protect the land and its plot holders from commercial interests, in 1914 Hartsdale Canine Cemetery was officially incorporated. As a result, the rural, pastoral wonderland was soon equipped with much-needed iron fences and walking paths, giving it the look and feel of a human cemetery. To passersby, it was nearly indistinguishable from a human graveyard; that is, except for the signage atop the front gate's entrance: HARTSDALE CANINE CEMETERY, 1896.

Throughout the 1940s and beyond, Scheu and Lassen's enthusiasm breathed new life into the cemetery. In addition to updating the infrastructure, they followed through on implementing a new business model as well. Rather than wait for the economy to bounce back, Scheu and Lassen increased their pool of potential plot holders by lowering prices. Hartsdale was hardly returning to the days of wood-shingle markers, though their decision served to democratize pet burials in the region.

"Prior to the Depression, the cemetery was really a place for pretty wealthy people," Martin admits. "But as a result of Scheu and Lassen's price reductions, more plot holders were people of middle-class means, people who were able to do this and wanted to do this."

Though the cemetery was now affordable to a growing number of people, there were still those who found it priced beyond their means. As a result, on more than a few nights, the Scheus and the

Lassens—both of whom lived on-site with their families—were awakened by sharp knocks on their doors. Upon answering, they'd peer out at the emptiness stretched before them, then glance down at their doorstep to find somebody's dead pet. In an effort to make good on the pet owner's apparent wishes, the pair would cremate the animal at their own expense, then spread its ashes on the cemetery grounds.

Though doing so may have had some effect on their profit margins, both Scheu and Lassen knew it was the right thing to do. As a long-time neighbor to the cemetery, Scheu had often observed Dr. Johnson's kindness toward pet owners, and he hoped to continue the tradition.

Another opportunity presented itself one evening as Scheu headed to Hartsdale's front gates to lock up for the evening. Upon reaching the gate, he was confronted by a man and a woman heading his way.

"I thought they were sightseers, and when I asked them to come back the next day, the woman began to cry," Scheu recalled. "She told me that her dog had died and that she and her husband had brought him such a long way. Looking over at their car I was astonished to see Utah license plates, and kept the cemetery open and arranged burial immediately."

These acts of kindness soon extended beyond Hartsdale employees and were often performed by pet owners themselves. During our phone conversation, Martin fondly remembers a Mr. Snyder, who, after burying his own beloved pet in the cemetery, saw to it that others had the means to do so as well.

"There was an old show called *The Millionaire* on many years ago," Martin recalls. "The basic premise was that a very, very wealthy man would send his representative around and give a million dollars to someone. The only concern was that they would never know where the money was coming from. Mr. Snyder wasn't quite that secretive about it, but he would pick pet owners he didn't know at all, and he would buy the plot, make sure they had perpetual care on that plot, and would take care of all the monetary expenses."

Judging from Mr. Snyder's home address, Martin had no reason to believe the man was wealthy, though his finances hardly kept him from performing his gesture — perhaps his own personal way of honoring a departed pet.

These acts of kindness resonated with Ed Martin Jr., bringing into sharp focus the many human benefits of a pet cemetery. To an outsider such as myself, the message was clear: if a place like Hartsdale brings out the best in people, then it's best for people to protect it.

It's a charge the Johnsons, Scheus, Lassens, and Martins have embraced for over a hundred years. In addition to the cemetery's 1913 incorporation, the land has recently become further secured by its place in the hallowed rolls of the National Register of Historic Places. Hartsdale Pet Cemetery historian Mary Thurston proved instrumental in helping the cemetery obtain the prestigious designation, a process that demanded Thurston submit an eighty-four-page application to the Department of the Interior. In it, she argued that Hartsdale was deserving of the designation because the cemetery served as "the first mass expression in American history of the belief that nonhuman beings are integral not just to the quality of this life, but to the 'afterlife' that follows."

It was a bold claim, and one that caught the ear of the Department of the Interior, as well as my own.

Though pets have often been credited with providing pet owners a myriad of health and wellness benefits, did they truly affect our spiritual well-being as well? Was Hartsdale's designation of land for departed pets, as Thurston argued, America's "first mass expression" of an evolving relationship with our animals?

Of course, other cultures had made this claim long before. For centuries, the Phoenicians and Chiribayas, among other ancient peoples, had gone out of their way to bury their dogs in a manner that rivaled even Mrs. Walsh's enthusiasm. Yet Thurston argued that Hartsdale Pet Cemetery is unique not because it's the world's first pet cemetery (it's not), but because it's *America's* first. Thus its preservation ensures that the story of America's love for its pets will long be embedded in stone.

∴

Throughout the 1950s and beyond, much of the work of embedding these stories in stone fell to Edward Martin Sr.—an established monument maker who, at the behest of Scheu and Lassen, agreed to create monuments and engravings for people's deceased pets.

"[Scheu and Lassen] had heard about my dad's reputation," Martin explains, "so the people at the cemetery would take down what people wanted on it—Fido, for instance—and the year of birth and death and whatever message they wanted. He would get that done, deliver it to the cemetery, they would install it, and whatever money was left over they would split."

The task seemed simple enough, yet on at least one occasion, Martin Sr.'s side project as a pet-monument maker caused more grief than solace. As a young boy, Martin Jr. recalled watching his mother, Bertha, tearing up upon stumbling across some of her husband's tracing paper for a soon-to-be-engraved monument.

"I don't remember its exact words, but it was something like, 'To my best boy' or 'My beloved boy,' or something like that," Martin explains. "And it also had the birth date and death date, which made it clear that the person had lived a very short life, maybe seven to ten years. My mother grew very upset upon coming across it, and at dinner that night she told my father, 'Don't leave that around the house anymore.' She told him she'd been upset all day as a result of it. My father told her it was for a dog, not a child—which helped a little—but being a family of pet lovers, it only took a little of the edge off."

Bertha Martin's mistake might have been made by anyone. After all, many of Martin Sr.'s pet monuments were almost indistinguishable from the human versions, a shift that had begun long before. Perhaps one of the cemetery's most revealing monuments is for a sixteen-year-old dog that passed away in September 1902. It reads,

BORN A DOG
LIVED LIKE A GENTLEMAN
DIED BELOVED

This clear act of anthropomorphism—the forbidden trespass of applying human terms for an animal—occurs again and again throughout Hartsdale and other pet cemeteries. Yet perhaps it is less a "trespass" than further confirmation of the sociological shift Thurston previously described. For some, by the turn of the twentieth century pets were no longer animals, they were family—and thus afforded the same rites and rituals as any other departed family member.

Of course, for the majority of the American population, human family members still came first. This was true for George Lassen, who passed away himself in 1961, leaving his business partner, Chris Scheu, as the primary owner of Hartsdale. Scheu retired soon after, passing all cemetery responsibilities to George's wife, Irene, who ran the cemetery for thirteen years before finding a suitable replacement.

After much searching, in 1974 Irene Lassen called upon the monument maker's son, Ed Martin Jr.—then a practicing CPA—to take a look at the cemetery's business model.

"She asked me to come up as an accountant and talk to her about what in today's world would be called an 'exit strategy,'" Martin explains. "However, after I came up, it became clear that her real motive was to do what Dr. Johnson's family had done to them."

What Johnson's family had "done" to Scheu and Lassen was to place the cemetery in capable hands at a fair price, ensuring that Hartsdale would continue to serve the next generation of pet owners. Though Martin didn't know it at the time of their meeting, Irene Lassen was hopeful that the young CPA might consider becoming the next director of Hartsdale himself. Despite Lassen's luring him to the cemetery under the guise of reworking a business model, Martin never felt tricked by her tactic.

"As I get on in age," Martin laughs, "I know this isn't the kind of job where you just put an ad in the paper."

Having served the cemetery for nearly four decades, Martin understands this better than most. It takes a special kind of person to run America's largest pet cemetery, one with the business savvy to understand the numbers and the compassion to understand the human heart.

Though pet cemetery director wasn't the career Martin initially sought out, it was certainly the one he grew into. His transition to co-owner of Hartsdale served as a fortuitous career change, granting him more time with his family while simultaneously allowing him to leave behind the stresses of the auditing world. In addition to his cemetery duties, the flexibility of his new job allowed him to teach accounting at the college level as well, a profession he came to love. Yet when in the cemetery, he functioned as an amateur sociologist as well, taking careful note of the many personalities filtering in and out of the cemetery grounds.

"When I came here, a newly minted CPA, I figured I knew everything there was to know about this business, but I really didn't," Martin admits. "I tried to do the classic things — looking at the demographics of who buries a pet and so forth. Most people think those who bury pets are old, wealthy women who never had children, and that their pets served as substitute children. Too often we classify these people in terms of age, race, religion, but it all goes out the window because there's only one common denominator on who buries their pets — pet lovers."

My family and I had always been pet lovers, which left me to wonder: what deep psychological sticking point prevented us from taking responsibility for Sandy's ashes? We had plenty of options, after all: we could have spread them, buried them, even shot them to the moon in a backyard rocket. Certainly anything would have been better than what we did do — leaving her dust to gather dust on the backroom bookshelf.

I adjust the phone, ask, "So what are the benefits of burying in Hartsdale? Who does it help?"

"When you go to a cemetery you think about when your pet was younger and healthier, and quite frankly, it just gives people a good feeling," Martin explains. "Intellectually we know it's just a bunch of chemicals rotting away in the ground, but it brings a good feeling for the small percentage of people who bury their pets."

Martin recalls that as Irene Lassen handed over the cemetery keys, she offered him one last piece of advice: "Remember, those who choose to bury their pets do so because they *want* to, not because they *have* to."

It's a lesson Martin has kept with him for years: a reminder that people choose how best to say farewell to a loved one, and that others should always respect that choice.

Yet before leaving Hartsdale for the last time, Irene Lassen also revealed one final secret about the cemetery.

Every once in a while, she told Martin, *humans choose to be interred right here alongside their pets.*

"I'd never heard of that," Martin admits, "so I asked a lawyer friend to have a look."

Soon after, the lawyer informed Martin that according to New York state law, it was, indeed, legal to bury human cremains in a pet cemetery.

Though Hartsdale buries the cremains of only five to ten humans per year, it's a service Martin is willing to provide plot holders for a modest $200 — a fraction of the cost of internment in a human cemetery.

"My job here is to protect the plot," Martin explains. "And quite frankly, if someone came in before, and they were a loyal plot holder but they couldn't afford the two hundred bucks, I would have done it for nothing. It's essentially digging a little hole," Martin says. "And for these people it's the right thing."

When I offhandedly remark that Stephen King's book might lead some to believe otherwise, Martin is quick to dismiss the comparison.

"People who make light of our business are never going to bury a pet here anyway," he says. "And when people come in and say something that they think is going to make me laugh, I usually get a little offended."

He pauses, releasing a slight chuckle.

"Sometimes I take those kind of remarks personally," he admits, "but for good reason. Because the bottom line is this: my mother and father, as well as my mother-in-law and father-in-law, are all buried here in my pets' graves," Martin confides. "And if you want to know the truth," he continues, "there's an empty spot for me when my time comes."

∵

As our final phone interview winds down, I realize that though I now have a better sense of Martin's business, I'm still struggling to get a clear sense of the place. The pictures, I'm told, don't do it justice, so I rely on Martin's description instead.

"Tell me," I say, "what do you see out your office window right now?"

"Well, right now I'm looking out at trees and flowers," Martin says. Though a self-proclaimed perfectionist, Martin admits that for the moment, he likes what he sees, that he's proud of the place he's known for more than half his life.

"Of course, I strive to see this place without any flaws at all," he says, "so I'm the guy who looks for the piece of paper on the path or the cigarette butt, but . . . truly, this is really a beautiful place. I've got a great job," he says. "I come into work every day and I can visit my mother's and father's plots, and my wife's mother's and father's plots and . . . well, I know how lucky I am. How many people can go to work and have that kind of experience?"

Sweetening the deal further is that he works alongside two of his sons as well.

"We're pretty much all here," he laughs.

And as Martin has already explained to me, he plans on staying forever.

"Matter of fact, they're fixing up the plot for me now. Mowing it and so forth."

"What's it look like?" I ask. "The place where you'll be buried?"

"It's a very shady area," he says, "so shady that it requires a little attention because not everything blooms all year long."

He goes on to describe his own personal patch of land amid the pets, including his own former dog, Coach, and his grandchildren's fish.

"I get the feeling it's not going to be half bad," he chuckles.

Though I've yet to meet him personally, I get the sense that Ed Martin embodies wisdom far beyond what one might expect from an accounting professor/pet cemetery director. For him, life is more than number crunching and digging holes in the earth.

"You've taught me a lot about Hartsdale," I tell him, "but you've taught me a lot about life and death, too."

He laughs, shrugging off his wisdom like a true sage.

Before hanging up for the last time, I ask him what I ask everyone: what lessons he's learned, what pets have taught him over the years.

There's a long silence on the other end, followed by a clearing of the throat.

"It's not what the pets have taught me exactly," he begins, "but what I've learned from pet owners."

"And what's that?"

"We're all here to help others any way we can."

My mind immediately leaps to the acts of kindness previously performed by Dr. Johnson, Chris Scheu, and George Lassen, even the mysterious Mr. Snyder.

"For me," Martin continues, "helping others means giving people a place to bury their pets. And sure, it's not for everyone, but for those it helps, we're honored to do it."

The sincerity in his voice prompts me to begin blathering just how much I hope to meet him one day, how much I hope to see Hartsdale for myself.

"According to the map, Hartsdale and Eau Claire are only 933 miles apart," I joke.

"Well, swing on by anytime," he says. "I'll cut you a deal on the twenty-five-cent tour."

"Maybe I'll take you up on it," I say. "Thanks so much."

As I hang up the phone, I have no way of knowing that within a few months' time I'll have reason to make the trip to Hartsdale to say good-bye to a dog for good.

But for the moment I place the future on hold to focus on the lessons of the past.

I reach for my notebook, then jot down my fifth and final lesson, the one Ed Martin Jr. has learned and lived throughout his life.

LESSON #5: HELP OTHERS ANY WAY YOU CAN.

PART 2

.....

Lessons Lived

SIX

.....

APOLLO'S DEED

Dogs never bite me. Just humans.

—MARILYN MONROE

I meet Apollo the day before he's scheduled to die.

Earlier that afternoon I'd received an email from Eau Claire humane officer Bekah Weitz informing me of the dog's fate. If I was still interested in observing euthanasia, she'd written, then I was welcome to drop by.

The "still" wasn't quite accurate. In truth, I hadn't ever been particularly interested in witnessing such a thing, though following my ride along with Bekah a few months prior, she'd encouraged me to witness her most difficult of tasks. If I was truly committed to understanding our relationships with animals, she'd argued, then didn't I have to understand their hardships as well?

When she'd first floated the idea, my initial reaction was thanks but no thanks, that while I appreciated the offer I was afraid I'd have to pass. But a part of me knew she was right, that she was simply pointing me down a path I hadn't been brave enough to walk alone.

Over the previous few months I'd learned five essential lessons from people and their pets — teachings that ranged from the value of living our lives with hope to the importance of helping others. But I knew it wasn't enough to have simply learned them; I needed to experience firsthand what it meant to live with these lessons in mind, even when doing so proved difficult.

Okay, I relented. *Just let me know when you need me.*

And then I waited.

And then I waited some more.

As the summer wore on, my anticipation worsened. It was only a matter of time, I knew, before we were faced with a dog on death row. Equally haunting was the prospect of being called to action at a moment's notice. The uncertainty of it all—*Will it be today? Or tomorrow? Or the next day?*—began to wear a hole in my heart. How could I even enjoy a walk with Cici when I knew my phone might ring?

It wasn't the phone, but an email, that transformed my anticipation to dread. I now had a time and a place and a name—*Apollo*—all of which ensured that there was no backing out. Though I knew observing a dog's death was sure to further wear at the hole in my heart, I reminded myself that there were lessons to learn in a pet's final moments, if only we are brave enough to watch. With trembling fingers, I clicked a reply to Bekah's email, thanking her for the opportunity and promising to see her and Apollo the following afternoon.

∴

I can't wait that long.

I've hardly sent the email before realizing that if I am going to watch a dog die, the least I can do is try to understand how he lived. I don't have much time—nor does he—so I drive to the Eau Claire County Humane Association later that afternoon, take a deep breath, then knock on Bekah's door.

"Oh, hey," Bekah says as if she'd been expecting me. "What's up?"

"Hey. Are you busy?"

"No," Bekah sighs, wheeling her chair away from her stack of manila files. "I mean, yes, of course," she corrects, "but I'll do just about anything to get away from these cases for a while."

And then, without skipping a beat: "So, are you here to meet our dog?"

Our dog.

She leads me through the labyrinth of cinder block hallways, bypassing the crates and kennels of cats and dogs until we arrive at the creature in the second-to-last kennel in the row.

"Here he is," she says. "Meet Apollo."

I take my first look at the brindle-colored mixed breed, haunted by the knowledge that within twenty hours' time he will no longer be scratching at his cage. But he is now, offering us a friendly tail wag to boot.

"Hey, Apollo," I say. "'Nice to meet you."

Though he's been identified as various breeds—terrier, pit bull, even a boxer mix—Bekah believes he's most likely some breed of cattle dog, or a Plott hound, perhaps.

When I hear this last breed name leave her lips I am reminded of the only other Plott hound I'd ever known—Dorsey, who had belonged to my neighbors, and whose funeral I'd attended while home from college so many years before. Dorsey had been the gentlest of dogs, which makes it hard to believe that this dog now wagging his tail before me could be capable of killing a cat, as he's been charged.

Yet his paperwork confirms that this most recent cat killing wasn't even Apollo's first transgression. He'd allegedly bitten a woman the previous August, and to make matters worse, a second cat had been killed in his neighborhood the night prior to the killing that led to his capture. It's quite a rap sheet, and in accordance with the City of Eau Claire's dangerous dog ordinance—a two-strikes-and-you're-out policy—Apollo has struck out. After being deemed dangerous by the police department he was ordered out of the city. Yet his expulsion hadn't necessarily been his death sentence; that came later—once the local media grabbed hold of the story and reported on the "pitbull and terrier breeds" that had committed the heinous act.

In truth, a dog identified as a pit bull had taken part in the killing.

His name was Diesel, Apollo's partner in crime; both dogs allegedly lived together temporarily with a shared owner. The police report described "two knee high pitbulls," though the news report noted the terrier breed as well.

What most people don't realize—and what I, in fact, didn't realize until recently—is that the term "pit bull" doesn't describe any specific breed of dog but is employed as a descriptor that encompasses several breeds, including the American pit bull terrier, the American Staffordshire terrier, and the Staffordshire bull terrier. Yet when many of us hear the term "pit bull," we think not of the loveable Pete the Pup of *Little Rascals* fame but of the muscle-bound killers often portrayed in the media. While there's no question that pit bull–like dogs have, on occasion, been responsible for killing animals and even humans, pit bull advocates such as documentarian Libby Sherrill argue that the real problem isn't the pit bull itself, but an overzealous media anxious to capitalize on fears perpetuated by faulty stereotypes.

In her 2010 documentary *Beyond the Myth*, Sherrill cites several statistics that do much to prove her case, including information from Newslibrary.com, which revealed that "68% of articles reporting pit bull or pit bull 'mix' attacks mentioned 'pit bull' in the headline." On its own, this statistic may not seem terribly shocking, though more than a few eyebrows begin to raise when it's juxtaposed alongside another fact—that a mere 8 percent of articles involving non–pit bull dog attacks specify the breed in the headline.

Though no definitive answer can account for this discrepancy in reporting, one theory may very well be linked to another statistic Sherrill provides, courtesy of the Independent Data Collection Center: "92% of people believe pit bulls are portrayed negatively by the media." Given the aforementioned statistics on headline distinctions, we begin to understand why. How, after all, can we ever see the good in a dog when the media inundate us with the bad?

Despite knowing virtually nothing about Apollo or his breeding, when Bekah tells me he's not dangerous, I believe her. He certainly doesn't look dangerous—at least not toward humans—just anxious to go for a walk. We oblige him, snapping a leash to his camouflage-colored collar and letting him lead us toward the shelter's back entrance, past the chorus of barking dogs jealous of Apollo on his walk.

Trust me, I think as I peer into the cages, *you wouldn't want to trade places with him.*

As Bekah, Apollo, and I meander the grounds, I finally get around to the question that's been weighing on my mind.

"He did it, right?" I ask. "I mean . . . he's guilty. He killed the cat. There's no question, is there?"

"I don't know if it was Diesel or Apollo," Bekah explains. "I wasn't there. But in any case, the city deemed both dogs dangerous and expelled them."

"So where's Diesel?" I ask, glancing around the yard.

"Diesel found a new home outside the city," she says, "but they couldn't find a home for this guy."

"Why not?"

"Probably because Apollo's a bit older and uglier," Bekah says frankly. "Sometimes we can find homes for expelled dogs out in the county, and sometimes we send them to other rescues. But since this story made the news there's been some public outcry over the 'pit bull–type dogs' that killed this cat," she explains. "But as you can see, Apollo's not even a pit bull."

I don't know enough about pit bulls to say for certain, though upon reexamining the print version of the story, I confirm that the news does, in fact, describe Apollo and Diesel as "pit bull and terrier breeds," making no effort to distinguish between them.

Not that this excuses Apollo's behavior. After all, he is on the eve of his death because he killed a beloved family cat, not because the local news mentioned the phrase "pit bull." Yet I can't help but wonder if Apollo's fate might've been different had the news not mentioned the breed distinction, if instead it was reported that a "pair of dogs" rather than "pit bull and terrier breeds" committed the act.

Equally disconcerting to me is that while the police report made clear that both dogs were to blame, the pair face far different fates.

If they're both involved, I wonder, *why does one get condemned to death while the other enjoys a life outside city limits?*

Simply because one was older and uglier?

I can't help but draw comparisons to our own criminal justice system. If an equivalent event had occurred in the human realm, would a plea bargain have led to a similar outcome: one executed and another relocated? Further, would stereotypes have played a role? Race? Prior convictions? Age and physical features?

"So why tomorrow?" I ask, interrupting my own thoughts. "Why's tomorrow his day?"

"He's been here since Saturday," Bekah says, "but our freezer's full, so we have to wait until after the truck makes the pickup tomorrow morning."

I pause as I allow the seemingly arbitrariness of it all to sink in.

"You mean there's not enough room for his body in the freezer," I say, slowly piecing it together.

She nods. "Not until after the truck makes the pickup."

Despite its momentarily full freezer, the Eau Claire County Humane Association has proved quite successful in keeping animal euthanasia to a minimum. While the Humane Society of the United States estimates that somewhere around 2.7 million healthy dogs and cats are euthanized in shelters each year ("about one every 11 seconds"), the ECCHA does very little to contribute to that number. According to the ECCHA's 2012 statistics, of the 728 dogs received into the shelter that year, only 58 (8 percent of the total) were euthanized. Cats fared worse, with a 31 percent euthanasia rate; 377 of the total of 1,142 cats received that year were euthanized. While the numbers aren't as low as the ECCHA would like, they're both well below the national average.

For comparison's sake, just look to Troy, North Carolina's Monroe County Animal Shelter, which in 2012 managed a shockingly high 99 percent euthanasia rate, killing twelve hundred animals within a year's time, including 100 percent of cats and 98 percent of dogs. Even in the seventy-two hours leading up to their deaths (the state-mandated time period prior to euthanasia), the animals often endured conditions deemed "deplorable" by inspectors, forced to live out their final days in an environment that often lacked the bare essentials: food, water, shelter.

When breaking down the ECCHA's numbers further, I'm surprised to learn that of the 437 instances of euthanasia that occurred throughout 2012 (58 dogs, 377 cats, and 2 "Others"), only 44 animals were euthanized for reasons related to limited space. One hundred and sixty-seven were euthanized for "Behavioral Issues" (which is where Apollo falls), while the 48 percent that remained were euthanized for reasons of "Illness/Injury." I try to find a silver lining in the knowledge that nearly half of the euthanized animals weren't healthy to begin with. Yet I can't help but wonder, *Just how sick were they?*

As Bekah and I walk Apollo back toward his cage, a part of me wants to remind this dog of the very lesson Bekah taught me earlier in the summer: live your life with hope.

But it's a lesson that doesn't apply to Apollo. How can he live his life with hope when his death has already been determined? There will be no reprieve, no stay of execution, no pardon from the governor. No matter what I do or say or write, I know this dog is destined to die in less than twenty-four hours.

I take one last look at the kennel where he'll spend his last night: a cement-floored square complete with bed, a pair of fetching balls, and overflowing bowls of water and food.

Altogether, it's not a bad place, just *a* place, and one he'll leave only two times more in his life: one for his morning walk and then, a few hours later, for his fated walk to the euth room.

Before leaving him, I press my palm against the kennel door, hopeful that my familiar scent might be of some comfort to him the following day. He leans toward my hand, gives me a disinterested sniff, then curls into his bed. As we walk away, I notice the words "Cat eater" scrawled in the upper left-hand corner of the information sheet attached to his cage. It's his scarlet letter now, his crime made public to the world.

A few minutes later, Bekah leads me through the cinder block maze until we wind our way to a locked door opposite a chest freezer about a dozen feet in length.

She reaches for a key, unlocks the door, and allows me to enter.

"This is the euth room," she says, peering inside the fluorescent-lit room with the sky-blue walls as if seeing it for the first time. "It's actually a pretty nice room," she admits, "but we never do anything but euthanasia in here."

"Why's that?"

"Animals have some serious olfactory powers," she reminds me, "and they're going to know that animals die in here. Death has a scent. Anyone who does euthanasia for a living knows that no matter how well we clean this room, it still smells like stuff died in here."

In an attempt to keep from over stimulating the animals with too many smells, Bekah keeps close tabs on everything that enters the room.

"When an animal comes in here, we want it to be quiet and serene," Bekah says. "We don't want it sniffing around everywhere and getting all worked up."

Opposite a small table is a countertop that stretches the length of the room. Just above it are various wood-paneled cabinets, each with a label: SYRINGES, NEEDLES, HYDROGEN PEROXIDE, COTTON BALLS, and one I don't expect—CLAM JUICE.

Bekah notices the curious look on my face.

"It's to help the cats take down some pretty terrible-smelling meds," she explains.

I'm surprised to learn that clam juice makes anything smell better, though I dismiss the thought and keep my attention on Bekah, who continues her tour of the cabinets.

"All the stuff we use is in here," she says, opening and closing a few cabinet doors. "The chemical is called Fatal Plus, but it's actually sodium pentobarbital."

She walks me over to a drawer on the right side of the room.

"Over here's where we keep the log," she says, removing a one-inch-thick white binder labeled EUTHANASIA DRUG LOG.

"Sodium pentobarbital is a controlled substance," she explains, flipping through the pages, "so any euth tech like myself has to have a license, and it's all tightly controlled by the government."

I nod.

"We also use a premix for a tranquilizer."

"Premix?" I ask.

"Basically, it's a mix of xylazine and ketamine that we inject intramuscularly if we need to keep the animal calm. But we don't always need it. I euthanized five cats today," Bekah says casually, "and they didn't need any."

I try to pick my jaw up off the floor.

Five euthanasias? I think. *All before lunchtime?*

"I have to ask," I begin, "what's that like? What's the mental and emotional toll of euthanizing so many animals day after day?"

Bekah assures me that she doesn't actually perform this difficult duty "day after day." Nobody does. In fact, in an effort to avoid overburdening any one ECCHA employee with the job, the shelter has implemented a weekly rotation.

"There was a brief time when just me and another woman did all the euthanasia in the building. That was really hard because you just get stuck," Bekah says. "You get in this mind-set of just not caring about anything because you're trying so hard to compartmentalize your emotions. You even stop caring about the stuff you're supposed to care about, like going home and eating dinner with your boyfriend."

I'm reminded of the startling statistics I've seen on the abnormally high suicide rates of veterinarians, leading me to wonder if the same holds true for shelter workers. Especially those like Bekah, who, even if she doesn't do it "day after day," regularly fulfills the role of euthanizing a seemingly endless supply of animals.

"I've had days when I've had to euthanize fifteen cats," Bekah says, "and then, when I go back up front, the girl at the front desk says, 'We just got seventeen more cats today . . .'"

"So it's a wash," I say. "Some die so others can live."

"Sometimes you just need to make space, so you'll go through and look for the sickest of the sickest and euthanize them. And it sucks," Bekah says, shaking her head, "because probably they aren't even that sick. But you have to make a choice, so you're going to choose the sick ones and not the healthy ones."

Suddenly my "silver lining" theory begins to vanish.

Bekah recounts one particularly emotionally charged day when thirty or so cats were surrendered by a cat hoarder.

"Turns out all the cats had distemper," she explains, "so we had to do emergency euthanasia immediately upon intake."

It wasn't the number of cats that proved troubling to Bekah, but her own life reflected through her actions.

"There I was, seven months pregnant, euthanizing kittens this big," she says holding up her forefinger and thumb. "It was hard, you know? You can't look at the kittens and not think of it from a mommy perspective. Here I am killing all these babies," she says, pointing toward her midsection, "and then, here's my baby, just a few inches away . . ."

∴

Before leaving the euth room, Bekah explains where she will inject Apollo with the lethal dose of Fatal Plus.

"Right here in his front leg," she says, pointing to her own arm. "Dogs have a vein that wraps around like this," she explains, using herself, once more, as the diagram. "It should be quick. Usually under a minute."

One minute, I figure, I can handle.

"I doubt he'll move around too much, so we probably won't need the premix. But I'll have it ready just in case."

She explains that the Fatal Plus is essentially an overdose of a tranquilizer; how after it enters Apollo's bloodstream his brain will stop, then his lungs, and finally, his heart. All of it will be painless, she assures me.

"It sounds cheesy to say, but . . . it kind of is like they fall asleep," she says. "They get really high and then they fall asleep."

She ushers me out of the euth room, locks the door, then directs me toward the chest freezer I'd spotted earlier.

"And here," she says, lifting the lid wide, "is where we keep them."

I'm wholly unprepared for what I see next, though how does one ever prepare for so much death squeezed into such tight quarters? My gag reflex crowds my throat as I peer down at what appears to be a multicolored cat-skin rug. There are fifteen or so cats on the top layer, alongside a few small boxes containing other animals. The boxes offer the animal's identifying information, often accompanied by a grief-stricken frownie face scrawled in marker; my own frownie face comes as a result of the sheer number of dead animals stretched before me.

Who knows how many there are? Since my eyes glaze over, I can't even venture a guess. Nor do I want to. My weak stomach returns, and though I know these animals have accumulated for several weeks, upon seeing them for the first time, I can think of nothing beyond the image itself. This is the harsh reality of America's animal shelters; despite everybody's best efforts, not every animal makes it out alive. No longer am I considering the ethics of animal euthanasia—or the necessity—but simply the aftermath. And this is the aftermath—an entire freezer full of it.

In their current state—dead and forgotten—the animals leave me with the impression that they're disposable and easily replaced.

That can't be true, I think. *Surely someone once cared for them, right?*

Finding my voice, I ask, "You said you did five cats today?"

Bekah nods.

"Do you happen to know which ones?"

"Oh sure," Bekah says, peering into the freezer. "There's this one, and this one, and this one, and this one, and this guy under the other one."

She introduces me to each by thrusting a finger into their frozen furs.

Someone did *care*, I think, much relieved, *at least enough to remember*.

Bekah surprises me further by introducing me to each dead cat by name.

"This is Dora, and this one is Bittersweet, here's Beans, here's Sea, and the fifth one is . . ." Bekah begins, pausing over the body of the final cat. "Blossom, I think?"

"You know all their names," I marvel.

"Well, today anyway," she shrugs. "Not all of them all the time."

We leave the euth room and the freezer and start back toward the lobby.

"You know, it's not Blossom," Bekah says, referring to the fifth cat's name. "Now it's going to bug me."

She turns to Sara, the adoption coordinator working the front desk, and asks, "What was that last cat's name?"

"Dear Prudence?" Sara tries.

"No, Dear Prudence is still alive. It was in the same litter . . ."

She checks a wastepaper basket for a bit of paperwork, but it's not there.

"Well, the answer is in an animal log somewhere," Bekah sighs, admitting defeat. "Many years ago I thought I should be keeping track of all their names. Euth techs are weird like that," she says. "Some of us have collections of collars for the ones we really didn't want to have to do."

"How many collars do you have?" I ask.

"I have three," Bekah says.

"I have seventeen," Sara pipes up. "All cats. A lot of them I really fall hard for."

The following afternoon, as she draws Apollo's dose of Fatal Plus into the syringe, Bekah will explain to me the importance of naming every animal before it dies.

"We all believe that nothing should die without a name," she'll say. "Even if it's some awful, feral cat."

But for now—nineteen hours prior to that moment—all I do is

thank Bekah for the tour, for introducing me to Apollo, and tell her I'll see her soon. We say our good-byes, though I hardly make it back to my car before my cell phone begins to buzz.

I glance at my screen to see that Bekah has texted me a one-word message: OLIVE!

Olive, I think. *The fifth cat's name was Olive.*

I smile for the first time all afternoon.

∵

The next morning, I awake to a tremendous dread I don't know how to fix. My watch reads 7:00 a.m., which means Apollo has about six hours left to live.

Feeling anxious and helpless, I take to my backyard with the ax and prepare to chop firewood. It's the kind of mindless task I require, something to busy my hands and distract my heart as I try to steer clear of what's coming.

Yet with each swing of the ax my eye catches my wristwatch, forcing me to continually recalculate Apollo's trajectory toward death.

I begin searching the wooded area in my backyard for a few more logs when I notice a caged raccoon peering up at me. I freeze as my breath escapes my body. Getting a hold on myself, I crouch, then peer into the cage. Judging by the empty can of cat food clutched between the raccoon's paws, it appears my neighbor has lured him here, has trapped him here by choice.

The cage is so small that the creature inside can hardly turn around, and though I know my neighbor has no intent of killing it—that she'll likely just release it away from our homes—seeing it there, as anxious and helpless as me, makes me feel sick all over again.

A part of me wants to set it free, to release the spring door and watch it scamper back into the woods. I tell myself that by releasing this raccoon, I will actually be releasing a kind of alternative karma into the universe. That if the raccoon goes free, maybe I can retain some cosmic balance to even out Apollo's impending death. At such an early hour, it's easy for me to overlook what Kathie Schneider's experiences with dual disabilities have led me to understand about "fair shares" and cosmic balance. What I need most in that moment is a reason to believe that the universe *does* care—that it cares deeply—and that I am not nearly as helpless as I feel.

It's early, sure, but that hardly keeps me from pounding on my neighbor's front door. At the very least I want to tell her that the trap has been sprung, the raccoon apprehended, and that she needs to do something—anything—to ensure it doesn't suffer any longer than necessary.

I knock, and when she doesn't immediately come to the door, I just keep knocking.

∵

Five hours later I am there, in the euth room, as Bekah prepares the needles.

As she draws the Fatal Plus (a.k.a. "the blue juice") into the syringe, Bekah says, "It's sort of sad, but when you do this long enough, every time you see an animal, you also see a little number floating by."

Number? I wonder. *What number?*

"The rule for IV injections," she explains, "is 1 CC of Fatal Plus for every ten pounds of animal. So sometimes I'll see a forty-five-pound dog and think, 'Okay, so I'd need about 5 CCs to kill you . . .'"

I shudder. It's a terrible side effect of the job—forcing an animal lover such as Bekah to view animals in terms of CCs of Fatal Plus.

A knock on the door and Sara, the adoption coordinator, enters.

It's her week in the euth room as well, which means she'll be assisting in our task.

"We're doing Apollo first, right?" Sara asks.

"Whatever order's going to be easiest for you," Bekah replies.

Sara mulls it over, then says, "Why don't we do Apollo? I'll go grab him."

As she slips away, I find myself trailing behind her.

We begin our walk down the row of kennels, past the blaring radio, and the mop bucket, and the pack of barking dogs.

Along the way Sara grabs a pink leash, then walks casually to Apollo's cage.

"Hey, boy," she calls, her voice raising an octave. "Hey there, Apollo!"

She speaks in a way that makes it seem as if Apollo has just won the lottery. Her voice hits the high notes, so exuberant and full of life that despite the racket that surrounds him, Apollo looks momentarily at ease. He stands, wags his tail, and appears happy to see us.

Please, I think, *don't be happy to see us.*

I give him a pat on the head as he and Sara walk past the row of barking dogs one final time. He doesn't pay them any attention, and in fact, only slows once along the route to sniff a few cats in carrier cages right outside the euth room.

"Stay away from those cats," Sara warns. "That's why you're in the big house to begin with."

Sara directs him toward the euth room, and as she does, Apollo freezes. He lifts his nose, sniffs, and I think back to what Bekah had told me the previous day about the lingering odor of death.

I wonder, *Does his nose know more than he does?*

With a gentle tug, Sara leads him in. She kneels beside him, offers him a robust pet around the jowls and midsection.

"Who's a good boy? Who's a good boy?" she asks, and though the answer to that question is certainly debatable, in his final moments, I find myself wanting to give him the benefit of the doubt.

"Just don't let him bite me, okay?" Bekah says, reaching for a yellow squeeze bottle and dousing his front paw with rubbing alcohol.

There is no fanfare, no ceremony, just the routine insertion of a needle into a dog's front leg. I wince, though Apollo doesn't even react. He appears wholly disengaged from the process, perhaps a little bored by it. After a moment, he feels the wetness on his front paw and begins licking the insertion point.

"Good boy, Apollo, that's a good monkey," Sara coos.

Just outside the door, the cats in the carriers begin meowing, a chorus of yowls, though Apollo no longer seems to notice. He's grown woozy, but rather than lie down as I expect, he stands and wanders toward the corner of the room, then heads back toward Bekah when she calls for him.

"Can you lay down?" Sara asks. "Can we try to lay down?"

We.

A minute passes, then two, but Apollo does not lie down.

"Honey," Sara says, stroking his fur, "how can you be doing this?"

Another minute.

Bekah injects the premix to calm him, then adds the remaining Fatal Plus.

Sara kisses his head as Apollo finally slumps into her arms. He's not dead yet, but he's fading, slowly, his legs stiffening beneath him.

"He's got gorgeous fur," Bekah comments, running a hand across his back.

"What a nice brindle," Sara agrees.

They chat casually, appearing as disengaged as Apollo.

This, I think, *must be how they cope—distracting themselves from the reality of a beating heart soon to stop.*

At least that's how I cope, listening intently to the conversation and hanging on every word. My close listening is similar to the trick I'd tried the previous day when allowing my eyes to glaze over. Only now, I amplify my ears—heightening one sense in an attempt to dull the rest. I successfully lose myself in the chatter, at least until I inadvertently glance down at Apollo's chest to see that it no longer rises. His heart, too, appears to have stopped. Sara confirms this with the stethoscope.

Bekah readies the eighteen-gauge cardiac needle, inserting it between Apollo's ribs and into his heart as a surefire test to ensure that his life has ended. The needle wags, spins, repeats a figure eight.

"When an animal dies—well, when anything with a heart is dying—there's just a little bit of . . . irregular heartbeat," Bekah says, nodding to the bobbing needle protruding from Apollo's coat.

"So when you checked the heart with the stethoscope," I say, turning to Sara, "you didn't hear much?"

"It was just a 'lug, lug,'" she says, imitating the dragging sound of a car engine trying to turn over.

"A regular heartbeat is obvious," Bekah says, pounding her palms together in a careful rhythm. "A dying heart is more like 'err, err . . .'"

Their audible interpretations can't prepare me for the final heartbeat, which we observe together while kneeling alongside Apollo.

The cardiac needle bobs once, twice, then stops for good.

Though Apollo's death wasn't as quick as I'd expected, it certainly appeared painless. One moment he was simply sniffing about the room, and the next he was folded into Sara's outstretched arms, the brush of her lips atop his head.

As the needle turns limp, Sara gives Apollo one last kiss.

"Bye sweet boy," she says, and that is it—that is everything.

She waves good-bye and then leaves to assist with an adoption.

Bekah and I are alone now, staring down at the newly dead dog.

"So you gave the premix in the middle," I say. "Was that normal?"

"That was unusual," Bekah admits. "Usually the dog is too hyper, so we do premix to knock them out. But he was pleasant at the start, and it wasn't until the middle that he decided he wanted to be active. So I had to give it to him then."

I nod understandingly, then glance down at Apollo to see a slight movement from his muzzle, his nerves flaring like rapid fire.

"Don't worry, he's dead," Bekah assures, nodding to the unmoving cardiac needle. "But sometimes the brainstem will fire and things like this will happen. Once I even saw a chest rise up."

My hand is on his back—it's been there for a while now—and though he's still warm and his body feels much the same, it's clear his state of being has changed. My hand is no longer on a dog's back, but on the back of an object that was once a dog.

Bekah sighs, then reaches for Apollo's collar, which Sara unhooked and tossed to the tile floor in Apollo's final moments.

I think back to the previous day's conversation—how some euth techs hold onto the collars for sentimental reasons.

"So . . . what happens to his collar?" I ask. "On to the next dog?"

"No," she says. "Honestly, it seems wasteful to throw them away, but we do, because we feel they have bad luck."

"Do you mind if . . . can I have it?" I ask.

I'm not sure what provokes the request. Maybe it has less to do with Apollo's passing than my role in it. Though I am well aware of Apollo's actions — actions that ultimately cost him his life — I know also that Apollo was loved and cared for and likely still is, and the thought of tossing his collar into the trash seems an unfitting tribute. Every dog, even a "bad" dog, deserves to be remembered. I want to carry that burden for a while.

Bekah considers my request, then hands it to me.

"Sure," she says, "it's all yours."

I peer down at the camouflage collar, feeling its weight in my hands. For the past twenty-four hours I'd convinced myself that this would be hard — that all death is hard — but in truth, it hadn't been as ugly as I thought. The ugliness was mostly a result of my imagination turning a relatively simple procedure into something more complex. At least the science had proved simple; I was less certain of the emotional impact of what I'd witnessed.

Bekah crouches, picks Apollo up by his legs, and walks him toward the freezer. I hold the door for her, glancing down at our feet at the cats that continue to meow up at us.

"Bye, buddy," she says, adjusting Apollo along the right side of the freezer.

He's just a body now, quiet and empty. No spark, no anything. Though I witnessed his death firsthand, it's still hard to understand how a dog that, just twenty minutes prior, had wandered past that freezer is now being stored inside it.

"Well, now I've got to do these guys," Bekah sighs, bending to retrieve the cat carriers.

I hadn't realized these were the marked cats. That the same animals I'd heard meowing throughout Apollo's euthing would soon join him in that freezer.

Bekah's got a job to do — a difficult job — and so I leave her to it. I manage a whispered thank you before making my quick exit through the cinder block halls toward the foyer.

Before leaving, I spot Sara typing at a computer.

"Thanks, Sara," I croak, moving quickly toward the parking lot.

"Have a great day," she calls, all the usual formalities intact.

I walk zombie-eyed into the lot, where I spot Bekah's F-150 pickup parked alongside my car. I hadn't noticed it before, though I notice it now: Bekah's "I ♥ Dogs" magnet stuck to her truck's tailgate, a proclamation I know to be true.

Visibly shaken, I collapse into my driver's seat. Though I can't forget what I've seen, I remind myself that I've only seen the half of it. There is more to this story — a perpetrator and a victim — and to understand it fully, I know I need to learn about Purrl.

∵

It's easy to sympathize with a dog you've just watched die. What's harder is retaining that sympathy upon learning of the trespasses that led to his death. Which is exactly what I hope to learn three days later, when I knock on Scott and Sally Dawson's front door. They are the human parents to Purrl, the eight-year-old cat that Apollo and Diesel killed just two weeks prior.

I'm nervous, hesitant to intrude upon a grief so fresh. Nevertheless, I'm there, standing in their Stein Court driveway, just a little over a mile from my home.

After a few quick raps on the screen door I spot a man's silhouette coming toward me. As he steps into the light, the silhouette gives way to reveal sixty-six-year-old Scott Dawson, a bearded man in beige shorts, a red shirt, and white gym shoes with tube socks pulled high above his ankles.

"Hi, there," I say, offering him a vase of flowers. "I brought you these."

Scott takes the flowers and, for a moment, appears genuinely touched by the humble gesture. But his smile fades upon remembering the event that prompted me to bring the flowers in the first place.

"They're pretty," he says, walking them over to a table near the window. "Fragrant, too." He holds the vase out to me so I can take a whiff.

A moment later Sally enters the living room and introduces herself.

"He brought us flowers," Scott reports, running his fingers through his curly salt-and-peppered beard. "How nice."

Sally agrees, smiles, then offers me a chair while she and her husband take seats alongside one another on the couch directly across from me.

I return the smile, trying hard to find a segue that might lead us into what will undoubtedly prove to be a difficult conversation. Difficult not only because of the subject matter — or the rawness of the grief — but because I am just some stranger who has entered their home, just some young man who has plunked himself down in their chair and asked to hear of their cat. In the animal world, perhaps this sort of interaction might've been easier. A quick sniff, a bit of play, and we might be best friends for life. But in the human world, our relationship is more complex, and my encroachment into their lives is not without its complications.

If the tables were turned, I think, *would I be willing to talk with me?*

"Maybe we can begin by your telling me a bit about Purrl," I suggest, hoping I've hit upon the proper entry point. It seems that I have, at least for the moment, as Scott offers a half smile as he reflects on his beloved cat.

"She was such a peaceful cat," he begins. "And she liked dogs. We have a large dog next door and the dog just loved her. She got along with all of them."

Scott explains how he, Sally, and Purrl had lived in the Wisconsin countryside for years prior to moving to the city. And in all that time — as the young cat tromped through the swamps and the woods — she never ran into any trouble.

"It's ironic," he says, "because out there she could have been attacked by all sorts of things — bear and mink and fishers — but she lived in harmony with all of them."

Scott points past the sliding back doors just behind us toward a few pine trees near the edge of the house.

"She loved to wander around the pine trees here," he says, "and the patio, and underneath the chairs . . ."

Yet despite her familiarity with the place, and the safe feelings she'd likely come to know as a result of that familiarity, it was here—in this backyard—where she had her fatal run-in with Apollo and Diesel.

"I remember there were times when she'd be sitting on the steps here watching rabbits ten feet away from her," Scott continues. "There were two rabbits, and she'd just look at them. She didn't act aggressive or try to attack them or anything. In fact, one time I caught her next to a baby bird. She was just looking at it. She was that gentle of a cat."

Though both Scott and Sally are distraught over Purrl's death, it appears to have affected Scott the most. These days, when Sally goes off to work, the newly retired Scott feels a loneliness he's never felt previously. In the past, he and Purrl engaged in a daily routine—her meowing followed by his reply. It was a morning ritual he treasured, and a ritual taken away from him all too soon.

"I have a problem being home alone now," he admits. "In the mornings, it's just so . . . quiet."

It's a problem he can't shake. He's haunted by the memory of the viciousness of the attack, so much so that he can't even glance into his backyard without being flooded with the memory he'd just as soon forget.

"We're going to move," Sally informs me. "As soon as we can. We just can't live here with that memory."

∵

At a little past 4:00 p.m. on Tuesday, July 23, 2013, Apollo and Diesel escaped from their home and began running through the nearby neighborhoods. They trotted along, a riled pair, until spotting a flash of fur near the pine trees in the Dawsons' backyard.

According to a witness report, the Dawsons' neighbor watched from the safety of her window as the dogs tore through her backyard chasing after a cat. "The cat would get away but they kept chasing it and they each had a hold of an end of the cat," the report noted. "It looked like they were shaking it."

A second witness report confirmed the first, another neighbor testifying that she witnessed "two dogs tugging and pulling" on what she recognized as her neighbor's cat. "It looked like the cat was partially killed or already dead," the neighbor reported.

Around 5:00 p.m. Sally returned home from work to spot Purrl in the backyard alongside the pair of dogs. The dogs appeared exhausted, their chests heaving as they panted beneath the backyard pines. In her police statement, Sally wrote that at first she thought "[the dogs] might have been playing" before realizing her cat was dead.

"I was a crazy person that night," Scott admits. "I was not in control. She had control," he says, nodding to Sally, "but I was not in control."

He describes loading his .357 pistol and walking outside, standing just fifteen feet from those dogs and preparing to shoot.

"I could have done it," he says, nodding to his wife, "but I was persuaded not to."

Sally was not against killing the dogs, per se, but remained fearful of what might occur if the police pulled up and spotted her husband armed and preparing to shoot.

"It was gross," Scott says, shaking his head and repeating his mantra: "I just was not in control that night."

Sally remained in the yard while Scott entered the home to return the gun. He reappeared a few minutes later, clutching a baseball bat in one hand and his checkered flannel shirt in the other. He handed the bat to Sally, then covered Purrl's body with his shirt.

The dogs watched curiously from their place just a few yards away from their kill.

"The brindle, the larger dog, never came at me," Sally says, referring to Apollo. "But the smaller one got tired of waiting and wanted to come and get something to eat."

"So you just stood out there with a baseball bat?" I ask incredulously. "You and the dogs?"

"I don't know what I was thinking," Sally admits, shaking her head.

"I was foolish, because they could have come at me, but I felt like I would have killed them before I let them touch Purrl again."

Sally pauses, a faraway look sweeping over her eyes before she refocuses her gaze.

"So we guarded her. It took an hour at least before the police got there."

"You just stood there staring those dogs down for an hour?" I ask.

"Yeah," she agrees.

Sally explains that there were moments during that hour-long wait when the dogs occasionally left Purrl's body to run through other neighbors' lawns. They left, returned, then left once more, likely from the excitement spurred as a result of the police and animal control officer's eventual arrival.

At some point following Purrl's death, Apollo and Diesel continued their romp through the neighborhood, gaining the attention of a young girl who spotted them while peering down from her second-floor window.

"Dad," she hollered, "the dogs are here!"

Fearing for her own dog's safety, she rushed outside, snatched the dog, and hustled back toward the house. Her father reported that Apollo chased both his daughter and her dog, later commenting that his daughter was "visibly upset" as a result of Apollo's actions.

Yet soon the dogs returned once more to the Dawsons' backyard.

Scott and Sally mince no words in describing the grisly scene, though it's still difficult for me to imagine: the pair of grief-stricken humans standing guard over their dead cat while her killers watch on.

"It just burned in my mind," Sally says, "the picture of Purrl and the dogs."

"It was an unbelievable picture," Scott agrees. "Like it was posed. Two dogs lying like this and then Purrl . . . all within four feet of each other. Statuesque. It was so freaky knowing how Purrl had often played with dogs, but this was not a playing thing."

Scott's head dips, and Sally rests her right hand on his knee.

What's most frustrating for Scott is his belief that Purrl died in vain, that the dogs who killed her had no business being in his neighborhood given their past transgressions — including an alleged incident involving a human the previous August, not to mention a neighbor's cat that had been killed the previous night.

"Mistakes and accidents happen," Scott says, "but the accident that happened was that dog [who allegedly attacked the human] was allowed to live. That was more than an accident."

Accident or otherwise, the state's dangerous dog ordinance gives little latitude when it comes to dogs that injure or kill. According to Wisconsin state statute 174.02, a court can order a dog euthanized if the case meets two criteria. First, the dog must have caused "serious injury to a person or domestic animal on 2 separate occasions off the owner's property, without reasonable cause." Second, the dog's owner must be notified of the first offense prior to the occurrence of the second event. In Eau Claire, there is a bit more wiggle room in that a dangerous dog can also be expelled from the city limits, thereby sparing the dog's life.

This was the fate Diesel received, though it was not Apollo's.

∴

Three days prior to my meeting with the Dawsons, as Bekah, Sara, and I crowded around Apollo in the euth room, I admit that I did not think of Purrl, but only of the life fading before me. If I had been witness to Purrl's attack, surely I would have felt differently. However, after hearing the Dawsons' side of the story — often in disturbing detail — it became easier for me to understand the city's decision to euthanize Apollo. In truth, they had little choice. There were ordinances and statutes in place, and since Apollo — deemed dangerous — failed to find a new home, his options became severely limited.

The day before his death, as Bekah, Apollo, and I took our final walk together, I tried hard to imagine a narrative that might allow that dog to appear innocent.

Perhaps Diesel had done the killing, I reasoned, *or some other dog.*

Maybe, I thought, *Apollo had simply been in the wrong place at the wrong time with the wrong breed descriptor attached to him.*

However, the Dawsons' story—coupled with a careful study of the police report—makes it difficult for me to imagine a conceivable scenario in which Apollo was anything but guilty. There were too many witnesses, too many transgressions.

Nevertheless, just how much guilt are we comfortable leveling against a dog?

When I ask the Dawsons who's to blame, Scott's answer surprises me.

"Partially I blame the city," Scott begins, "because the dogs should have been put down. One's down now, but the other one should be, too," Scott says. "You got two involved in a crime. One didn't just look while the other bit. They *both* bit. It's simple logic. Put both dogs down."

Though I have yet to share with the Dawsons my own role as witness to Apollo's death, I breathe a sigh of relief in learning that they have at least been kept abreast of the outcome. I'm not certain Apollo's euthanasia provided much in the way of closure, though Scott seems to believe it's a good first step.

While Sally and Scott are in complete agreement that both dogs violated the city's dangerous dog ordinance, they differ in their views on justice.

"I'm satisfied that one of the dogs was euthanized," Sally says. "That was a gentle, painless death and more than Purrl got."

In addition to blaming what Scott views as a lax dangerous dog ordinance, he also blames, in part, the dogs' owner.

"A dog can only be as good as its owner," he says simply, throwing up his hands. "That's really all there is to it."

The human-pet relationship is indeed complicated, one structured within a firm hierarchy and contingent upon issues of both nature and nurture. While there are many benefits to pet ownership, one drawback to inviting a dog or a cat into our homes is that by doing so, we become responsible for that animal, charged with deciding how and when—and in what context—we allow that dog or cat to act naturally. As Bekah Weitz previously explained to me, despite our best efforts to domesticate these animals, when adopting a dog or a cat, we often forget we are adopting a predator as well. Despite our nurturing, the predatory instinct remains in the domesticated animal's DNA. When we watch a cat play with a string, for instance, we forget that perhaps we are actually watching that cat become a better predator. Likewise, when we tug on a rope with our dog, our attempt at play might be interpreted as training for the creature on the other end of the rope.

This is true of all dog breeds, and Scott agrees that despite Purrl's tragic end, he has no interest in breed-specific legislation aimed against pit bulls or terriers like Diesel and Apollo.

"I don't mind any kind of dog that's taken care of," Scott says. "A dog gets vicious because it's allowed to and because it's part of its nature. And when they pack up," he says, staring out at the pine tree again, "that's when they get into trouble. You get two running together and then they see something on the run—a rabbit, or a squirrel, or a cat—and they think, 'Let's go get it.'"

"That's nature," Sally agrees.

"Sure," Scott says, turning to his wife, "but that's not nature in the city. In the wild that can happen, but not in your freaking backyard."

Rather than advocate for a citywide breed ban, Scott hopes the city council will reexamine the dangerous dog ordinance's two-strike policy. But he hopes dog owners are better held accountable as well.

"This never would have happened with responsible people," Scott says, fanning his hand toward his neighborhood. "There are six dogs within a hundred feet of this house and Purrl never had a problem with any of them."

∵

The Saturday following the attack, the Dawsons took turns digging a burial plot on the edge of a woods in their friends' field thirty-five miles south of town. When they'd dug the hole to the proper dimensions, Scott lowered his cat's body into the ground. He laid her to rest wrapped in his flannel. The Dawsons buried her alongside her favorite toys, including a stuffed animal owl named Owlie, which Purrl often cuddled with as she slept peacefully on her chair. Scott's connection with Native American culture led him to believe that burying Owlie was more than merely burying a stuffed toy; he was burying a sentry who would continue to look over his cat.

"We really had a nice funeral for Purrl," Sally remembers, though their comfort wouldn't last.

In the days following Purrl's death, both Dawsons would experience interactions they couldn't quite explain.

"I'd hear her coming up the steps," Scott says. "I'd hear her bells, her collar."

Sally nods, then opens her mouth to speak.

"I know how this sounds," she starts, "but I have to say it because . . . well, I don't know what I perceive in this world in terms of life-forms and energy, but given the violent death that happened right here, I'm going to use the world 'haunt.'"

She pauses before continuing.

"It felt like Purrl's spirit was around here for a while, or her energy, or something," Sally explains. "Because I swear to God, I got up on the morning after we buried her and I heard her. She called. Just like she always did in the morning. At first I thought, 'Gosh, I'm being emotional.' So I get my robe on, I come out, switch on the light in the bathroom, and I hear her again," she says. She heard Purrl a third time as well, before deciding, "This is ridiculous."

Sally explains that sensing Purrl's presence became even more ridiculous a few nights later upon feeling a cat-sized shape disrupt the balance on their bed. There was nothing to see, but Sally felt a Purrl-sized weight shift between the sheets separating her and her husband.

"You hear about things like this and you're like, 'Yeah, right,'" Sally says. "But I have to say, I've experienced it."

When asked if they could offer any advice to grieving pet owners, the Dawsons describe what not to do: namely, try to replace what's missing.

After a well-meaning family member offered Sally a cat, Sally found herself bristling at the thought.

"I was like, 'Don't offer me a cat when my cat just died.' It hadn't even been a week yet. I'm not looking to fill a hole," she tells me. "I just want to mourn the death of Purrl."

Scott nods. "I've had a harder time overcoming this death than the deaths of my family members," he admits. "I've probably had fifty people die in my family in various ways and yet this . . . it's going to be hard to never not see her lying there with those two dogs. I'll never get that out of my sight."

Sally takes a more philosophical approach.

"Life and death aren't two different things," she tells me. "Death is just part of life and vice versa. You can't have one without the other. We're all going to go through it at some point. I didn't like what happened to Purrl—the way it happened—and I wouldn't have chosen it for her. If given a choice, I would've chosen what the dog received—a peaceful, painless transition. For that, I envy the dog owner."

Though Apollo's euthanasia had taken longer than expected, it had appeared peaceful. And now, just days after Apollo's death and weeks after Purrl's, both animals are finally at peace.

But the Dawsons are not—at least not yet.

I thank Scott and Sally for their time, and as I walk out the front door and onto their drive, I begin to wonder if perhaps Bekah's first lesson—*Live your life with hope*—extends beyond the animal world to folks like the Dawsons, who lost so much so terribly.

As I watch them disappear behind the closed door, I wonder if Scott and Sally can still find room for hope in their lives.

Of the many gifts Purrl gave them, did she give them hope as well?

SEVEN

.....

BINGO WAS HER NAME

Happiness is a warm puppy.

— CHARLES M. SCHULTZ

A few weeks after my visit to Bob's House for Dogs, forty-seven-year-old Emily Townsend was faced with a terrible choice. For the past few months, her beloved dog Bingo — a four-year-old Labrador-Chesapeake mix — had endured an onslaught of health issues, the combination of which had dramatically diminished the dog's quality of life. Chief among them was a genetic ACL disorder that affected both of Bingo's back legs, making it difficult for the dog to walk. There was no denying Bingo's suffering, though Emily's decision as to whether to euthanize was further complicated by her dog's relatively young age.

"Bingo's been a medical disaster from beginning to end," Emily had confided in me. She and I are colleagues, and over the years we'd grown accustomed to swapping dog stories in the hallways before class. Yet prior to her admission on Bingo's poor health, I'd had little knowledge of just how dire her dog's situation had become.

As Emily explained, even if she were willing to shell out the $8,000 necessary to cover the cost of a pair of knee surgeries, there were other expenses to consider as well. Such as the year and a half recuperation time, which would require Bingo — and by extension, her caregiver,

Emily—to be restricted to the bottom floor of their home throughout the recovery, a less-than-ideal situation for all involved.

Yet neither the economic nor the personal costs deterred Emily from the surgeries. What deterred her was the knowledge that even if the surgeries proved successful, Bingo would never again be able to run or play.

"How do you tell a dog not to run?" Emily had asked me. "How do you tell a dog not to play?"

In August, while standing outside my office door, Emily filled me in on the decision she'd ultimately reached. How, after exhausting all other options—including regular visits to a specialized veterinarian located seventy miles to the west—she'd come to the conclusion that the best she could do for Bingo was to let her go.

During a hallway run-in two months after Bingo's death, it was clear to me that Emily was still trapped in grief's icy embrace. Bingo's death had proved to be a traumatic experience for her, though the trauma had less to do with the death itself than her role in it, of being placed in a situation that demanded she make an end-of-life decision for her dog.

"Anyway," Emily said, wiping a few stray tears from her cheeks as we stood in the hallway outside my office door, "I'm not sure I'm ready for a new dog yet, but . . . keep your eyes open. You know, in case you run across anything . . ."

As I soon learned, Emily wasn't interested in just "anything." Having been the human companion to four wonderful dogs, her past pets had set the bar quite high. As we continued chatting, she began painting a portrait of precisely what she was looking for: a cat-loving, female black Labrador.

"I'll keep my eyes open," I agreed, though I was hesitant to do so. After all, every pet grief book I'd read had warned against the outsider keeping his or her eyes open too widely for a replacement pet. Pets cannot be replaced, the books warned, a sentiment confirmed by Sally Dawson in our conversations about Purrl.

Nevertheless, since Emily had approached me, I convinced myself that I wasn't the one applying the pressure, that I was merely acting as a friend.

Maybe she just needs someone to help her take the first step, I reasoned, and so I took it for her.

I entered my office, and after a quick search of the adoptable dogs at Bob's House, my first step turned into a leap.

I jumped from my chair, peeked into the hallway, and spotted Emily chatting with a colleague just a few offices away. Clipping down the hall, I whispered into her ear, "I think I found your dog."

∴

In the following morning's August swelter, my eighteen-month-old son Henry and I accompany Emily to Bob's House. We've reached the dog days of summer, which seems appropriate given our task. But I've also reached another personal milestone — my wife's first day at a new job, which means it's my first day at a new job as well, that of full-time father.

"Henry, get back here!" I call as he begins chasing the dozen or so skittering dogs across the concrete floor. We've hardly entered Bob's House before becoming the epicenter of chaos, which hardly surprises me. Over the past few months, this has become our modus operandi, chaos no longer a possibility, but a guarantee.

Thankfully, Bob's House thrives on chaos, and Henry is more than happy to contribute his own special brand. Yet if my son wasn't there to stir things up, I realize, the place might've seemed almost subdued.

Something has changed, I think as I peer around the house.

Though I can't quite put my finger on it, I reason that this slight change in atmosphere isn't the result of a change in the dogs' demeanors, but a change in the dogs themselves. Most of the dogs from my previous visit appear to have found homes, thereby opening up new spaces for other new-old dogs in need. Though it's always hard to say good-bye to her pups, there's nothing Amy Quella likes more. After all, saying good-bye means someone else is saying hello — proof of a successful adoption.

Though I recognize few of the furry faces that surround me, all the permanent residents remain, including Pete, the miniature poodle with a penchant for sitting on laps, as well as the trio of German shepherds, all of whom are off howling in a separate room. The only dog I specifically notice not in attendance is Warren, the hospice dog I'd watched snoozing in the sun two months prior.

When I inquire about him, house manager Nikki informs me that he's passed on, though she doesn't appear distraught by the loss.

"Warren was just old," she explains with a kind smile. "We knew he wouldn't last the summer."

Nikki's demeanor reminds me that when a pet passes at an appropriate age, his or her death can feel a bit less tragic. However, when the opposite is true—when a pet passes prematurely—the passing can often feel far worse. Not only did Bingo's young age make Emily's decision to euthanize all the more difficult, but it also added guilt to the milieu of grief she now feels.

"I don't know if a shelter will even allow me to adopt again," Emily had confessed to me in the hallway the previous day. "I mean, I put down a four-year-old dog!"

She'd said it as if she'd done so without cause. As if she'd simply tired of having Bingo around, which couldn't be further from the truth. If she'd tired of anything, it was the emotional exhaustion brought on by dedicating several months of her life exclusively to her dog: driving to and from vet appointments, preparing elaborate meals, and worst of all, keeping an unblinking eye on Bingo's decline, taking every step of the journey with her.

I'd assured Emily that given the circumstances, it seemed inconceivable that a shelter might turn her away.

"For Bingo, it was a quality of life issue," I'd reminded her. "You spared her a life with little quality at all."

My argument failed to persuade, though after sharing with her the cat-loving, female black Lab named Molly whom I'd found on the Bob's House website, Emily agreed to allow herself another chance to make a new best friend.

Meddling matchmaker that I am, I'm anxious to witness the first moments of this budding friendship, which is probably why I ignored all better judgment and deemed it a good idea to release a one-and-a-half-year-old into a house overflowing with dogs.

It'll be a tail-wagging good time, I'd told myself on the drive over, glancing at Henry in the rearview as he plotted the chaos soon to come.

Though I try to maintain my role as fully engaged journalist, my role as floundering father takes priority. Henry and his newly formed pack pull me away from Emily and Molly's introduction, demanding instead that I give chase to the chase that has developed throughout the house.

Amid the shrieks and howls (Henry's) and the barks and woofs (also Henry's), I overhear Amy introduce the two.

"Here's our girl," Amy says to Emily.

Meanwhile, half the house away, there's my boy, engaged in a game of tug-of-war with a tail that doesn't belong to him.

"I'm going to count to three," I warn, but my threat is so toothless that even the dog in need of assistance appears unconvinced in my ability to save him. He's right to doubt me. After all, what have I done to earn his trust, except unleash the fury of a tail-pulling, two-legged creature into his home? I am not the solution, but the problem, the guy who—for the first time in his life—is trying to navigate the dual role of father-journalist and failing at both.

As I embrace my current role (i.e., as I pry Henry's fingers from the dog's tail), I pick out a few phrases from Emily one room over—"good dog," "sweet girl," "I wish they were all like her."

When Henry finally collapses on a doggie bed on the opposite side of the room, I take advantage of the momentary calm to get to know Molly myself.

"Hey, girl," I say.

Molly directs her attention toward my voice, then wanders from Emily's side to greet me. Next, she puts her tail at risk by giving Henry a sniff on the doggie bed before ambling back to Emily.

The dog knows how to work a room, I think.

As it turns out, so does Amy. Though there's never a moment in which Amy officially accepts Emily's adoption application, at some point the conversation shifts from hypotheticals to practicalities.

"When do you think I can take her home?" Emily asks.

"Well, she's got an afternoon vet visit," Amy says. "But sometime after that."

"That sounds wonderful," Emily gushes, turning to Molly. "And we'll bring your baby home, too, won't we?"

Fit snugly into Molly's mouth is her "baby," a filthy plush bunny that, by the looks of its mottled fur, has probably outlived any breathing rabbit on the planet.

Emily tries hard to maintain her composure, but pure happiness seeps through.

It's a joy for me to see her joy, particularly since I've seen her grief as a result of losing Bingo.

I know it's time to take our leave, so after successfully wrangling Henry from his pack, I offer my farewells.

"Thanks, Amy," I say, and then, turning to Emily, add, "I'm so happy for you."

But Emily doesn't hear a word I say. She's already lost in puppy love, and my voice is no match for Molly's eyes.

∵

Later that evening, after giving Emily and Molly a few hours to get acquainted, I return to my interloping. Though I am clearly the third wheel in the relationship, Emily allows me my trespass, inviting me over to see Molly in her new environment. I agree to the invitation and slip from my car at a little past 8:00 p.m. on that summer evening, walking up the tree-lined street toward Emily's house. I make my way to the door, preparing to knock, though my fist freezes at the sight of their silhouettes through the screen. The pair are spread across the living room floor, just two former strangers thoroughly enjoying one another's company. I'm hesitant to interrupt their bliss-filled moment, but I do, eventually, and watch as the human silhouette jumps to her feet.

"Come in, come in," Emily says, waving me toward her. "Can I get you something to drink?"

I decline (or think I do), but Emily's already back on the floor alongside Molly before I even get the words out.

"Look who's here, Molly," Emily says. "It's our friend B.J."

I take a seat on the floor opposite Emily, my hand instinctually moving to the scruff of Molly's neck.

Molly glances over at me approvingly, then lifts her head a few inches higher as if to confirm she's the lady of the hour. Which, of course, she is—proof of which is seen in the wide array of dog toys that have already become scattered throughout the living room.

"So how's your new home, Molly?" I ask.

Though I hardly expect an answer I get one, Emily swooping in with her best Molly impersonation.

"Well, we took a nap," Emily begins, "and we went outside, and I've got all my toys out, as you can see."

"I can see," I laugh. "And you sure seem to have a lot of toys," I remark, glancing first at Molly's spread, then at the nearby toy box overflowing with a dozen or so more.

"I gave a lot of Bingo's toys away," Emily confesses, returning to her normal voice, "but I held on to a couple of her favorites. We've got the falcon," she says, introducing me to a plush toy beside my knee, "and the cow's in the other room. Oh, and we like the dachshund and the squirrel a lot."

I'm uncertain which "we" she's referring to: Emily and Molly or Emily and Bingo. There's a slippage in this particular "we," a momentary morphing in which former dog and current dog appear to be reunited, at least in Emily's head.

Before I can press her on this point, the "we" immediately returns to Emily and Molly, and any momentary conjuring of Bingo seems to have dissipated.

"...and we went in the backyard," Emily says, continuing her Molly impression, "and we've been on two walks, even one with the neighbor dog."

"Sounds like you two have had a full day," I say.

"We have," Emily agrees.

I turn my attention back to Molly, look her straight in the eye, and ask, "Is it true that you can shake?"

"Oh, she can shake," Emily confirms, though rather than prove it by accepting my extended hand, Molly collapses on my lap instead. "She can," Emily insists, "but mostly she's a big snuggler. Except for that poor nose . . ."

At Bob's House earlier that afternoon, Molly's nose had become the subject of much discussion. From what I could gather while liberating dogs' tails from my son's grip, Molly suffers from a case of discoid lupus, an autoimmune disease that has left her nose with a chipped-paint look. I'd overheard Amy mention to Emily that they were treating it with prednisone—a steroid primarily used for inflammation and allergies—and Amy was confident Molly would shake it in no time.

Yet Emily seems to have interpreted Molly's discoid lupus as just another plus. A dog with a special need fulfills Emily's own special need—to give care to others.

"She just has so many strikes against her," Emily says, staring deep into Molly's eyes, "it could have made for a difficult adoption." Though Molly's medical issues aren't as severe as Bingo's, she seems to suffer from just as many of them: lupus, Lyme disease, not to mention the usual wear and tear brought on by advanced aging.

"It's nothing," Emily shrugs, "at least compared to the things I've been through. I'm used to giving meds three, four, five times a day. And I'm used to special foods and diets. In fact," she says, pausing before continuing, "one of the reasons I chose to get an older dog is because my own medical condition isn't so great. My knees are bad, and I have chronic Lyme's myself. So I understand where she's coming from."

"You complement each other," I smile.

"We're a perfect fit," she agrees.

While Molly's various health issues wouldn't have proved an asset to all prospective pet owners, Molly is proof that the human-animal bond is stronger than society's "perfect" dog stereotypes. After all, Molly isn't perfect—what dog is?—though her physical impairments make her all the more perfect for Emily.

My mind leaps to what Amy Quella had taught me during my first visit to Bob's House earlier that summer, the lesson she herself had learned from her dogs:

Don't judge a book by its cover.

It's a lesson Emily knows well.

As she and I overwhelm Molly with belly rubs, the conversation veers to Emily's childhood, her early adulthood, and finally, to her history with dogs.

"We always had cats growing up," Emily says, "but I started getting dogs when I was about nineteen . . ."

"What prompted the change of allegiance?" I ask.

Emily turns serious and, in a voice just above a whisper, informs me that she got her first dog shortly after being the victim of a violent assault.

"I've always lived alone, and I liked living alone," Emily begins, "but after the assault, I was fortunate to live with some people, and those people just happened to have a kennel. They bred Akitas, which are pretty hard-core guard dogs."

I nod knowingly.

"But to me they were always just so sweet," she says, her tone lightening. "I lived with those people for about a year, and when I moved out, they let me take one of their brood bitches. She was six years old and done breeding. I named her Tomoesan—Tomoe for short—and she and I became inseparable."

Despite the assault, Emily persevered through her undergraduate studies, taking up residence with Tomoe in an apartment directly above the Joynt, one of Eau Claire's most famous watering holes.

"It's very unusual to be a college student and find a place that will let you have a dog, let alone a seventy-five-pound Akita," Emily says. "But it was awesome. For me, it felt very safe. The Joynt was my living room, and my apartment was the only place I've ever lived that had enough bookshelves for all my books. That dog, and that place, they gave me my life back."

Next came Roxie, a pit bull–chow mix, who performed a task quite similar to Tomoe's—appearing threatening enough to make Emily feel safe.

"People would cross the street when we came by," Emily explains, which at that point in her life was exactly what she wanted. "Roxie and I had moved to Colorado by that point, and we'd always go hiking in the mountains together. It was so peaceful."

Emily's third dog was a Labrador named Ally. She'd been rescued from a hoarder's home, and thus she, much like Bingo and Molly, had special needs herself.

"She was bone-thin when I got her," Emily recalls. "And she just wouldn't leave the house. It took us about six months before she would even go on a normal walk with me. In fact," Emily says, standing, "I just came across a picture of her a few days ago . . ."

Emily leaves Molly's side long enough to dig through a nearby box. She hands the photo to me, and I smile at the sight of a younger Emily hugging her bone-thin dog just outside a Colorado drugstore.

"That's when I fell in love with Labs," she remarks, peering over my shoulder at the picture.

"And finally," she sighs, "there was Bingo." A slight waver returns to her voice as she returns to her place on the floor. "My sweet, sweet Bing . . ."

She gives me the abbreviated version of Bingo's medical history—starting with her leg issues and moving on to her host of other ailments.

". . . and then there were her allergies, which were almost uncontrollable," Emily continues. "We'd give her Atopica, but that can hurt a dog's immune system. Then again, if we *didn't* give it to her she'd chew herself constantly. You'd run into places where she'd just chewed herself to these bare patches," Emily says, shaking her head. "And then there was the Lyme disease, which meant we had to put her on antibiotics, but then that started interfering with the Atopica . . ."

Just hearing Bingo's medical history proves exhausting, and I can hardly imagine what it must've been like for Emily to witness her dog's decline day after day.

"It sounds like your life was pretty . . ." I pause, searching for the right word, "*consumed* for a while."

"Oh, it was," she smiles. "But you know me, I have to have something I can take care of. The yard's nice, and students are nice, but it's not the same. I don't have kids," she reminds me, "so they *are* my kids. They get the same care, the same treatment."

And probably a few more toys, I think, smiling as I peer at the overflowing toy box beside me.

"I have to say, though," she admits, "I'm not as good a person when I don't have a dog. I'm just not. I'm meaner to my mom, I'm crankier, I don't have the patience, I turn inward. The world looks really ugly to me when I don't have something beautiful in my life."

"I know what you mean," I agree.

Fatherhood has taught me many lessons, chief among them the value of finding beauty in everyday living. After spending a year or so elbow-deep in diapers, I've come to reevaluate how I spend my time and with whom. And much like Emily, after all that caregiving, I've begun to understand that caring and giving often go hand in hand. I've also learned that caring for someone else—be it a dog or a son or a houseplant—has a reciprocal effect: the love we put in we get out.

It's an equation Emily understands, though for her, love comes in the form of forgiveness.

"Part of getting another dog was about giving myself permission to forgive myself for not being able to save Bingo," she admits. "When your dog is older it's much different. With Bingo, it wasn't ever a question of age; it was about what was left to try. The questions were always, 'Do we try this or not?' and 'What are we not thinking of?'"

Emily brushes a wisp of loose hair as she tries to fight back the tears.

"And then there's the feelings of recrimination," she continues. "There were so many things wrong with Bingo, but part of the problem was that she was overweight, and of course, that was on me. People are always nice about it, but that sort of thing falls back on the owner. She loved her food, and at the end, there was so little that she loved that she got whatever she wanted," Emily whispers, tearing up. "That's not going to happen here," she says, turning a stoic gaze toward Molly.

"You know, Emily," I begin, playing the part of the friend, "some might say that it wasn't the weight that killed her. That it was the joints, the legs, the Lyme disease, the allergies. That it was all of it."

"Yes, but weight's a factor that can trigger other things," Emily reminds me. "Her prognosis for recovery was so much lower."

I shoot her a raised eyebrow. Though this may be true, it's hard to blame Bingo's wide range of ailments on weight gain alone.

"It's not necessarily rational," Emily agrees, "but . . . sometimes we like to take responsibility for things we can't change. And I'm a big responsibility taker."

"Maybe to a fault," I smile kindly.

"She shouldn't have weighed as much as she did," Emily reiterates. "That was something I could have controlled but didn't. There was a lot of self-anger after that," she adds. "I'm not good at forgiving myself, and so . . . Molly's my redemption."

For Emily, Molly seems to serve as a stand-in for many things — she is the embodiment of love, loyalty, and forgiveness, to name a few. But she is also a dog, and a senior dog at that. Which means that despite the many virtues Molly can bring to Emily's life, she cannot expand her own. If life is a dog, she is fast approaching her own tail end.

"I know this is hard," I begin, "especially given what you've been through with Bingo, and since you've just met Molly and all, but . . . I think I've got to ask you a hard question."

Emily nods, readying herself.

"It seems that the difficult truth about adopting a ten-year old dog like Molly is knowing, on some level, that in the best-case scenario, you'll probably only have four or five good years together. And so my question is, Is it worth it? Is your abbreviated time together worth the looming grief?"

I expect a bit of pondering, a bit of mulling it over perhaps, but Emily's answer comes like spitfire.

"Oh yeah," Emily nods firmly. "I knew the risks when I fell in love with this girl."

Molly leans back, meeting Emily's eyes, and as they stare at one another, I do my best to fade into the backdrop.

Embracing my invisibility, I use the opportunity to examine the scene that surrounds me, taking careful note of the dog toys, the food bowl, and, for the first time, Emily's apparel.

"For the record," I say, interrupting the lovefest, "I should note that you're wearing a 'Life is good,' T-shirt. Coincidence?"

"I've got about twenty 'Life is good' T-shirts upstairs," Emily laughs. "But this is the first time I've worn one in about six months," she whispers, continuing to gaze at Molly. "Today was the day I decided life was still good."

After giving her new-old dog one final pet, Emily says, "Follow me. Let me show you the shrine for my girls."

Molly and I trail after her up the stairs, turning right at the landing and entering into a book-filled study.

There, on the back dresser—alongside several piles of books—are the ashes of two of Emily's former dogs. It's not a shrine in the conventional sense (there are no candles, no incense), but it's certainly a testament to Emily's love for these animals. Passersby would hardly notice, but given the lack of dust on the dresser, I get the sense that Emily visits here often.

"These are the old girls," she says, nodding first to Tomoe's urn, then to Roxie's box.

"Here's a picture of us at the Great Divide," she says, pointing to a frame of a young Emily posing atop the scenic landscape with Tomoe's thick body in her arms. I can't help but notice that the exact same picture is framed across the room as well—Emily's love for Tomoe seemingly confirmed in duplicate.

"And here's Roxie," she says, nodding to the box of ashes. "Here's a photo of her playing in one of our favorite streams."

She shares a few stories of each dog before ushering Molly and me into the room across the hall.

"This is Molly's room," she says. "Or *our* room," she corrects.

Though the study appears to be a book-lover's paradise, this room really rouses the bibliophile in me. Emily's books are everywhere: scattered on desks and shelves and stacked halfway to the moon. My eyes scan the titles—a habit no bibliophile can resist—until Emily draws my attention to a pair of small white boxes atop one of the shelves near her bed.

"And here," she says, "are Ally and Bingo."

A few stones gather in a small dish atop Ally's box, while leaning against Bingo's is a picture of a black dog swimming with a stick protruding from her mouth.

I stare at the boxes and begin thinking back to my first dog, Sandy, whose ashes still remain in that copper tin on the backroom bookshelf, as they have for well over twenty years. Since my family and I never quite knew what to do with them, I call upon Emily for her suggestion on how best to honor a dead dog.

"What do you plan to do with them?" I ask, nodding to the ashes.

She pauses and, for the first time all evening, hesitates to answer.

"You're going to think this is weird," she begins, "but . . . whatever happens to me, I want my girls with me."

I nod, assuring her I've heard this plenty of times, that she's not alone in wanting to share her final resting place with her pets. As proof, I tell her the story of Ed Martin Jr., who has already picked out the plots for him and his family in the shadiest section of Hartsdale Pet Cemetery.

"It just feels right to me, . . ." she begins, then interrupts herself midway through her sentence. "Oh, I almost forgot!" she says, moving hastily toward the bedroom's walk-in closet. "I have to show you the blanket."

Prior to our moving upstairs, Emily's and my "Molly-as-redemption" conversation had segued into an unexpectedly deep exchange on fate and searching for signs in the universe—both topics I've pondered on more than a few sleepless nights.

"Sometimes you see these connections between your dogs," Emily had told me. "For instance, when I got Ally, I learned her original name was Roxie, which was, of course, my previous dog's name. And now with Molly, you see this Christmas collar?" she'd asked, running a finger across the green collar with the peppermint-striped bones. "Well, Bingo has a blanket with nearly the exact same design! Remind me to show you."

I'd forgotten, though she'd reminded herself.

And now, as I stand in Emily's walk-in closet, I watch as she digs her way past boxes and clothes in search of Bingo's blanket.

"Here it is!" she says at last, handing it over to me.

I take a look, then compare it to Molly's collar.

The pattern *is* nearly identical, a coincidence that Emily reads as a clear sign from the universe.

"Of course, you can always find some coincidence," Emily concedes as the three of us loiter in the closet, "but I like to think that this is Bingo's way of telling me it was time. I think she's tired of watching me be so sad. She's got better things to do than look after me."

Emily smiles, scratching Molly behind her ears.

"Isn't that right, girl?" she asks. "It's time to move on, huh?"

We leave the closet, but before leaving the room, my eyes fall to a can of pepper spray sitting prominently on Emily's bedside table.

There is still fear here, I think. And for good reason, given the violence Emily endured so many years before. Though I've never observed Emily to appear fearful of anything, the pepper spray seems to serve as proof that even after all these years, residual effects from the attack remain. Though if the evolution of Emily's dog-breed selections is any indicator, perhaps, over time, her fear has lessened.

As we sat in her living room half an hour before, Emily herself had acknowledged the trend.

"Somewhere along the line, I went from adopting these big, badass dogs to the gentlest, sweetest dogs I could find," she'd told me. "Something changed."

As she and Molly follow me back down the stairs, what "changed" suddenly hits me.

No longer does Emily need a dog to look after her, I think; *now she needs a dog to look after.*

It's a reversal that seems only natural in a karmic world, a world of cosmic balances in which the universe regularly throws us a bone (or in this case, a matching pattern) to help us make sense of life's serendipity.

As we reach the foot of the stairs I turn to face the new best friends.

"Listen," I say, "thank you for allowing me to be the interloper to your happiness. This all just worked out perfectly for you two."

"Sometimes you ask the universe for something and it gives it to you," Emily agrees, keeping one hand pressed firmly to Molly and opening the front door with the other.

After giving the dog one last pet, I wave good-bye to Emily and head toward the darkened street in the direction of my car.

"Come on, Molly," Emily whispers, "back inside, sweet girl."

As I watch them go, I reflect on past lessons, as well as a new one.

Though it may indeed be wrong to judge a book by its cover, perhaps judging a dog by her collar isn't so bad. At least in this instance: when the collar gives comfort, and the dog gives comfort, and everything given is returned in kind.

EIGHT

.....

THE BIONIC DOG

Every dog must have his day.

—JONATHAN SWIFT

Body parts are everywhere—legs to my left, hands to my right, and a thin layer of plaster dust coating the workbench before me. No, this is not Dr. Frankenstein's laboratory, just the back entrance to the Winkley Company, a reputable 125-year-old orthotics and prosthetics manufacturer situated a mile or so from my home. While their work with humans is impressive enough, unsurprisingly, my interest lies with the animals.

Though Winkley employees by day, by night Traiden Oleson and Terry Kufner represent two-thirds of Forward Custom Design—an animal orthotic company they founded in 2012. It's a small venture—one that takes up residence in the back room of Winkley's after hours—though don't be fooled by its humble origins. I'm already familiar with their crowning achievement—the Bruiser Cruiser—a four-wheeled little engine that could for a dog that doesn't believe in can't. I'm anxious to meet the men behind the inspired device, and as I enter through Winkley's back door to spot the surplus of hands and legs, I know I'm getting close.

"Excuse me," I call to a man hard at work reshaping a prosthetic. "I'm looking for Forward Custom Design?"

"Oh, sure," the man says, removing his safety glasses. "Terry's right over here."

I walk into the adjacent room to spot Terry Kufner, a blue-jeaned, bib-overalled fifty-two-year-old with a grin as wide as his workbench.

"You're the guy who wants to see how it's done," Terry says, offering me a hearty handshake.

I am indeed, and without wasting a moment more on small talk, he leads me to his latest creation, Bruiser's new and improved Cruiser—the Bruiser Cruiser 2.0.

"The Gurklises wanted something that disconnected from the harness," Terry explains, reaffirming what Tammy had told me a few weeks prior. "So I just put a couple of rods in here," he says, nodding to the metal platform just above a pair of black wheels. "The rods slide right out like this," he demonstrates, "which should help Bruiser sit a little easier."

"New wheels, too," I notice. "You're moving up from the rollerblade wheels?"

"I stole these off my grandson's toy tuck," Terry laughs, touching the treads on the wider wheel attached to the new cruiser. "He wasn't even playing with it, and I thought, 'These would be perfect...'"

In addition to the disconnect feature and the new wheels, Terry also has plans for one final innovation—repositioning the original rollerblade wheels to the platform's front and back to assist Bruiser's balance.

"So you use toy truck wheels, rollerblade wheels, pretty much anything," I observe, running my hands over the new cruiser. "It sort of seems like pet orthotics is still a bit of a Wild West."

"It is," he winks, "but experimenting's the fun part."

Terry's first experiment in the world of animal orthotics occurred fifteen years prior, when the owner of a goat with a bum leg approached Terry for a solution.

"I just fashioned a little thing out of PVC," Terry says modestly. "It wasn't much."

Nevertheless, the PVC dramatically improved the goat's mobility, and by extension, its quality of life.

In the years that followed, Terry continued receiving requests from pet owners in desperate need of an alternative to surgery.

Surely, pet owners began to reason, *there must be another way.*

Over a few rounds of beers, Terry, Traiden, and a coworker helped pioneer this "other way." They recognized this region's need for animal orthotics and, given their experience on the human end, figured they were the men for the job.

"So we formed a company," Terry smiles. "We all threw in a few hundred bucks and we've managed to recoup it, so I guess that makes us a real business."

As Terry gives me a guided tour of the workshop—from vices to kilns to hand tools—he continues to stress the many similarities between human and animal orthotics.

"The animal anatomy is obviously different," Terry says, "but it's the same type of thing. On the human side, we do a lot of stifle braces, which is basically a knee brace for when you blow out a knee. And it's the same for a dog."

He leads me to a shelf of stifle braces and then begins taking me through the variations between models. Some braces provide flexibility, he explains, while others provide stability.

After examining one of the more elastic braces, I ask, "So what's the difference between a stifle brace and an Ace bandage?"

"Well, for one, these are expensive," Terry jokes.

Though, of course, it's more than that. The braces also have the added benefit of being individually constructed to meet the wearer's specifications. As a result of careful casting and shaping, each wearer (human or animal) is ensured a perfect fit.

As Terry continues his rundown on stifle braces, we're joined by Traiden Oleson, the fresh-faced, thirty-three-year-old member of Forward Custom Design. Tammy Gurklis had previously described him as "young and enthusiastic, a lot like you." Upon meeting him

I see that he is the far better dressed version of me, complete with a white polo shirt tucked military style into his beige slacks.

He introduces himself, though our introduction is cut short by the sound of a dog collar jangling near Winkley's back entrance. I glance up to spot Gretchen, a German shepherd mix, entering the workshop alongside her owners, sixty-seven-year-old Bob Johnson and his wife, Elsbeth. Traiden greets them, then ushers Gretchen off the slick concrete floors and back outside onto the grass. Terry and I follow them into the sunlight, watching as Gretchen's back legs drag as if weighed down by an invisible force.

We've just barely made it outside before the dog buckles, regains her footing, then buckles again.

"Hey, girl," Terry says, strolling over to examine her right hind leg. "How ya doing?"

Gretchen's eyes flash toward him, though Terry doesn't flinch.

"Don't worry," Bob says, "Gretchen's never gone after a person."

"Until today," Terry jokes.

Bob offers to retrieve a muzzle from his vehicle, though Terry waves off the offer. "I've been at this for two years now," he says, "and so far, no bite marks to speak of."

Until today, I think.

A few feet from the action, I take my place alongside Elsbeth, watching as Bob, Terry, and Traiden mull over their options for Gretchen.

"So what brings you here today?" I ask Elsbeth.

It seems obvious—her dog's back legs—though as I'm soon to learn, there are no obvious answers when dealing with pets.

"Well, we thought she had hip dysplasia," Elsbeth tells me, "but now the X-rays are showing us that's it's more in the knee."

"So you're considering a brace, then?" I ask, rattling off my newly acquired knowledge.

Elsbeth nods.

After a few minutes of observation, we return to the workshop, where we're soon joined by the third member of Forward Custom Design, who takes to a stool and positions himself near Gretchen's tail. Terry strokes the dog's head, calming her, as his coworker raises the platform on which Gretchen stands. Once she reaches the proper height, the man on the stool reaches into a nearby bucket for a roll of plaster of Paris and then begins wrapping the material upward from the bottom of Gretchen's back leg to her thigh.

"I sure am glad I saw your article in the paper," Bob says, referring to a recently published story on the success of Forward Custom Design's Bruiser Cruiser. "Because to be honest, we were getting pretty concerned about her."

In the few brief minutes I've spent with Gretchen and the Johnsons, I can already sense Bob's need for a solution. He's frustrated because his dog is frustrated; he's pained because she's pained.

Bob's spirits were buoyed upon reading the news article championing Bruiser's success. *If Forward Custom Design could find a fix for Bruiser*, he thought, *perhaps they might find one for Gretchen as well.*

On this July afternoon, Bob watches anxiously as Traiden tries to do just that. He kneels alongside Gretchen's hindquarters, studying them carefully.

"It looks like that leg really wants to turn in," Traiden observes, tracing the bend of her bone with his finger.

"It varies at different parts of the day," Bob says. "Sometimes she'll run around like a fool, but other times . . ."

He trails off, and I glance up to spot him swallowing hard.

"If this works the way I've seen it work for other dogs on your website," his voice quivers, "then this is going to be a lifesaver. Because . . . I don't know what else we can do with her."

Over the past year, the men of Forward Custom Design have become quite familiar with the high stakes involved in their work. Time and again, desperate pet owners call on them to work their magic, though their success is always linked to the severity of each pet's situation. While Terry and Traiden take pride in their successes, they also know the sting of defeat. Thus, when Bob informs them that an orthotic solution could prove to be a "lifesaver," Terry and Traiden know he means it literally.

The men work hard, and within five minutes' time, the first step in creating the stifle brace is complete. The quick-dry plaster has formed a perfect mold, allowing the coworker on the stool to reach for his utility knife and slit along a cut-off strip before prying the plaster loose. Gretchen peers down at her newly freed leg while the coworker walks the mold to the opposite side of the room.

"This is what we do on the human side, too," Terry explains to me. "The same exact thing. Make the mold, then create the cast from it. Add the joint dummy, make a few modifications with the polyethylene, then add our Velcro closure system to make it easy to slip on and off."

The entire process takes about a week, Terry says, at which point Gretchen and the Johnsons will return to give it a try.

Before leaving, Bob's asked to select which transfer papers he wants coloring Gretchen's brace.

"Pick something nice so she can show off at the dog park," Terry suggests, walking the man over to several rolls of waxy paper to choose from. The rolls feature stars, hearts, butterflies, and an array of colors, among various other designs. It's an extravagance Bob has little need for—all he needs is a fix—though he settles on a yellow sunburst color. Terry nods, cutting a small sample that he clips to the paperwork.

"That'll be good," he agrees. "It'll really pop."

Before leaving the workshop, Bob reaches into his wallet and hands Traiden a couple hundred-dollar bills—half the total price of the brace, and a fraction of the cost of surgery.

"I'm so glad I heard about you all," Bob repeats, sliding his wallet back into his pocket. "If the vet had his way, Gretchen wouldn't be with us a whole lot longer, and . . . well, you see what she's like. I just don't want to part with her yet."

"She's got everything else going for her," Terry agrees. "Just a bum back leg."

Bob nods enthusiastically, grateful for the ally.

"I've asked the vet so many times, 'Is she in pain?' and all he ever says is, 'Well, dogs hide pain pretty good.'"

"It's about quality of life," Terry says. "Can you improve a dog's quality of life? With a brace like this, I think you certainly can."

"I sure hope so," Bob sighs, offering us his first smile of the afternoon.

He shakes our hands before carrying Gretchen to the backseat of his vehicle and settling into the driver's seat alongside Elsbeth.

As we watch them pull out of the lot, Terry says, "Next week at this time that dog will be standing straight up and thinking, 'Hey, this is pretty nice.'"

"If that's true, then you guys really are miracle workers," I say. "And if you are," I continue, "and you come up with some kind of orthotic to keep my dog from barking incessantly, be sure to let me know."

"Oh, we already have," Terry laughs. "It's called a shock collar."

∴

The following week I return to the back entrance of Winkley's just in time to watch Gretchen begin circling in a grassy space a few yards from the lot. She's wearing her sunburst-colored stifle brace, though even with its added support, it doesn't appear as if she'll be loping around the dog park anytime soon. My heart sinks as Terry's prediction proves wrong. Gretchen is not standing upright, nor does she seem to think her brace is "pretty nice." Bob and Elsbeth stand supportively alongside their dog, their faces rigid as Gretchen's brace fails to stabilize her hip, which we've now learned is the true crux of the problem.

In her final months, my first dog, Sandy, suffered from a similar flaw in design. Though my parents often referred to her "weak back legs," they were actually referring to her hips. Her legs were fine, though much like Gretchen, over time her hips had worn away. It's a common problem for dogs, one often attributed to arthritis, degenerative myelopathy, Cushing's disease, or simply a deterioration of the joints. Yet despite the regularity of the ailment, treatment proves difficult. There is no cure for growing old or wearing out one's body. As a result, many dog owners—my parents included—"fix" the problem by taking it upon themselves to serve as constant caregivers. Through the winter and early spring of my first-grade year, I watched my mother and father carry Sandy back and forth from her beanbag chair to the lawn several times daily. Even then I recognized their sacrifice as an act of love, and judging by the concerned looks passing between Bob and Elsbeth, I get the sense they'd gladly do the same for Gretchen.

But the point of the brace — the point of visiting Forward Custom Design to begin with — is to avoid such measures. The question isn't whether Bob and Elsbeth are willing to go to these backbreaking lengths for their pet, but if they should. That is, if it's in Gretchen's best interest for them to do so. When determining a pet's health, the unknown variable in the equation is to what extent the animal's advanced age — or in Gretchen's case, injury — is linked to quality of life. Is the pet suffering, and if so, to what extent? The pet owner's inability to come to a definitive answer is one of the more unexpected frustrations of pet ownership. While many of us are familiar with the frustration that comes from slipper chewing, we're less prepared for the frustration we feel when we learn we've been cut off. That despite our years of loyalty, we will never truly know our pets the way they know themselves. Thus, when left to decide if it's time to say our final farewell to a pet, we rely mostly upon observation and intuition, neither of which promises conclusiveness. This level of uncertainty has long plagued Bob. If he only knew the degree of Gretchen's discomfort, he says, his decision might be easier.

I watch as Terry and Traiden begin troubleshooting the brace — examining their orthotic closely before turning their attention to Gretchen's joints and hips. But even after their thorough examination, they remain perplexed about how to correct what nature has done to her.

As Gretchen stands and tailspins again, we all begin coming to terms with the difficult truth: the hip is the problem, and there's no easy fix for a hip.

"It's not working real good for ya, huh, babe?" Bob says—an admission that deflates all our hopes further.

To ease her anxiety, Terry and Traiden unstrap the brace, then step back to study Gretchen as Gretchen studies them.

"What if we tried an elastic strap?" Traiden suggests.

"Something that wraps around the thigh," Terry nods.

After a bit more orthotics talk, Terry and Traiden slip effortlessly into veterinary speak. They discuss Gretchen's drop paw, her range of motion, her quality of life. They speak of joints and muscles and bone. As I watch them, I realize that these are not merely businessmen trying to find a quick fix. These are animal lovers desperate to find a solution for folks in desperate need of their help. As the men of Forward Custom Design have learned, when it comes to pets, it's always personal, and it's made all the more personal when an animal's quality of life is at stake.

Bob's eyes fade into Gretchen's fur as a *What now?* look slips across his face. Meanwhile, Terry and Traiden continue to discuss their options.

"Well, let's go inside and put a strap on her," Terry says, breaking Bob's trance, "no sense in being hot out here."

We enter through the back door, Terry and Traiden excusing themselves to work on the strap while I take a seat beside Gretchen and the Johnsons.

Finally, Elsbeth breaks the silence.

"I was actually hoping it would be a lot better than that," she says.

Bob and I nod solemnly.

"The leg just keeps folding under," Bob says, leaning forward in his chair. "She's been favoring it for so long, she's got a lot of weakness up there."

Nobody blames the men of Forward Custom Design. The problem isn't a flaw in the brace, but the difficulty of bracing a hip so far gone. Both Bob and Elsbeth seem to understand it was a long shot, that the field of pet orthotics is still new, and that their dog is on the cutting edge of an industry that—much like Gretchen—is still struggling to find its footing.

As any pet orthotist and prosthetist will tell you, one of the primary struggles of this burgeoning field is related to the difficulty of design. Simply put, there is no one-size-fits-all model that encompasses the myriad of limitations for the myriad of species and breeds. When it comes to pet orthotics, what's good for the goose is not necessarily good for the gander. This doesn't mean that innovators such as Terry and Traiden need start from scratch with each animal, though certainly individual attention and—as their business name implies—custom design is required. But as Gretchen proves, not every disability has its quick fix, not every mystery its answer.

Panting, the old girl glances up at her humans.

"She has her good days and her bad days," Bob sighs, "but these days, the bad ones are coming closer and closer together."

∴

Traiden emerges a few moments later, hopeful he's come up with a solution. He holds a strap that, in many ways, resembles an Ace bandage, only with one end tied into a loop. He hopes the strap will serve as an assist when Gretchen swings her leg, allowing the motion from one leg to help stabilize and propel the other. It's a Hail Mary attempt, but Traiden and Terry refuse to give up without a fight.

After reattaching the brace, Traiden feeds Gretchen's leg through the strap, pulling the strap tightly over her hindquarters before Velcroing it to the bottom of the brace. Gretchen stands, appears puzzled by this latest addition to her contraption, and then slides once more to the floor.

Traiden leaves to search for an additional piece of Velcro, when I hear a familiar voice booming from just outside Winkley's back door.

"Come on, Monkeyhead," Tammy Gurklis hollers, "don't be a big baby!"

I smile at the sound of her voice. I haven't seen Tammy since my visit to Thorp a month or so prior, and I'm anxious to hear of Bruiser's progress.

"Excuse me for a moment," I whisper to the Johnsons.

I slip out the back door just in time to catch Tammy crouched a few feet from Bruiser, brandishing a McDonald's cheeseburger.

"Hey, Bruiser," I call, "how you been, boy?"

Bruiser looks up at me skeptically, perhaps a bit annoyed that I've interrupted his tryst with Tammy and the cheeseburger.

"Come say hi," Tammy says, waving Bruiser my way via the cheeseburger, "you remember B.J."

If he does, he sure doesn't show it. Instead, he keeps a safe distance, not even giving in to the temptation of his favorite afternoon snack.

"Hey, no, no, no," Tammy calls as Bruiser turns tail and bolts back toward the car. "Come here, pal! Come on! We're not going bye-bye yet. Don't you want to see the new Cruiser?"

"Yeah, Bruiser, aren't you excited for your new Cruiser?" I ask.

"He better be," Tammy says, "because he broke the old one."

"Really?" I ask, withholding a chuckle. "How'd he manage that?"

"Oh, he just snapped it," she shrugs, shaking the McDonald's bag to regain his attention. "He was in a little valley in the yard, and he usually jumps right over it, but this time . . . well, he didn't quite clear it."

I grin, imagining a pole-vaulter snapping his pole.

"But everything else is good?" I ask. "Aside from the busted Cruiser?"

"Oh yeah," Tammy agrees. "Everything else is good. In fact, Ken and I got a roommate last week. A woman I went to high school with thirty years ago. We hadn't been in contact with each other until three weeks ago, but she needed a place to stay, and she has a pair of dogs, so she's staying with us for a while."

Typical Tammy, I think with a smile. *Always willing to open her home to a person (or pet) in need.*

Bruiser is continuing his shimmy toward the car's back axle when Winkley's back door pulls wide and out spill Gretchen and her entourage.

Gretchen—now wearing a strap in addition to the brace—growls upon spotting Bruiser, prompting the bulldog to retreat even further beneath the car.

"Bruiser!" Terry calls out jovially. "What the heck are you doing here?"

In her best Bruiser voice Tammy replies, "What are *you* doing here?"

"Oh, I'm always here," Terry grins as Bruiser cocks his head at him.

Tammy, Bruiser, and I watch from the parking lot as Gretchen continues circling in the grass. She spins and spins and finally slides to the ground much like before.

"Well, that didn't do much good," Traiden sighs. "It's that internal hip rotation, I just don't think there's much we can do . . ."

As if angered by the dim prognosis, Gretchen turns and takes it out on Bruiser—issuing a few sharp barks.

Bruiser moonwalks toward the back of the nearest car while Tammy claps her hands, ignoring her own dog and encouraging Gretchen to give it another try.

"You can do it," she says. "You got it, girl."

But Gretchen does not have it, at least not yet. She's tired, irritable, and confused by her unwanted transition to bionic dog. The hard plastic presses against her fur, and though the brace is as perfect a fit as Cinderella's glass slipper, that doesn't mean Gretchen approves of it. Given the choice between nature's discomfort and humankind's fix, she seems to have chosen discomfort.

Terry removes the strap, the brace, then circles the dog alongside Bob, Elsbeth, and Traiden.

Still not ready to throw in the towel, Terry promises to continue talking it over with the team.

"We'll get our heads together," Terry says, "and give you a holler when we come up with something."

When, I think, taking careful note of his words. *It's not an if, but a* when.

Bob nods, then helps Gretchen back to her feet.

"The braces are new and they're strange," Tammy whispers to me as we watch Bob lead Gretchen back toward the vehicle. "It takes a lot of encouragement. Bruiser was just terrified of his Cruiser at first," she says, "but after a while, he started coming around to it."

As Bob hoists Gretchen into the backseat, I'm reminded once more of all the days and nights I'd watched my parents perform a similar task for Sandy. Not only is it a gesture of love, I now realize, but it is the gesture pet owners make when they believe there's another corner yet to be turned, another chance at recovery. It's a gesture with a message attached, one that reads, *We don't believe in can't.*

Still, as Bob shuts the back door and makes his way to the driver's seat, I can't help but notice the hopelessness etched into his face. Elsbeth, equally disappointed, takes her seat beside him.

"It can be done!" Tammy shouts as the Johnsons drive away. "Have faith, folks! Just have faith!"

∵

While Traiden sets to work on braces for a few other dogs, Terry leads Tammy and me to Winkley's back room to focus his attention on Bruiser.

"You busted this up pretty good, huh, boy?" Terry says, taking a look at the mangled Cruiser. "Oh well, we'll get you fixed up, no problem." He reaches for a screwdriver and begins removing the rollerblade wheels from the broken Cruiser, inserting them onto the new one.

As he works, Tammy and I begin to catch up, though we've hardly said two words before a foul odor permeates the vast room.

"Bruiser!" Tammy accuses, waving her hand in the air. "You stinkpot!"

Bruiser, looking sheepish, shrinks behind the nearest chair.

"And you hardly even ate your cheeseburger yet," she says. "After that, you're really going to stink up the car."

It's an inevitability that hardly deters Tammy from feeding it to him, however, and this time, when she holds out the greasy burger, he gives himself fully to the temptation.

"Anyway, as I was saying before we were so rudely interrupted,"

Tammy says, shooting her stinkpot the stink eye, "we've got this new roommate now, and her two dogs, plus we got a new kitty, too."

What's that bring the count to? I wonder.

"Now, I know what you're thinking," she says, "but remember, none of these new additions are permanent. The dogs will leave once our roommate closes on a home, and the kitty, too, is only temporary. Just until we figure out who her new lucky owner will be."

"So just to recap," I say, "you've added three new pets into the fold over the past three weeks?"

"Three weeks?" Tammy laughs, shaking her head. "Goodness, no. That was just last week!"

I wonder what next week might have in store for Tammy—a horde of hamsters, or a brood of hens? Surely, she'd turn none of them away. But before I can ask, Terry enters the room with his Bruiser Cruiser 2.0 in tow.

"Okay, here we are," Terry calls. "The new and improved model."

Tammy runs her hands over it, clearly fascinated by the orthotic.

"Look, Bruiser! It's got the quick release like we hoped for," Tammy says, pointing to the pair of metal rods that, when pulled, separate the platform from the chest brace.

Bruiser appears unimpressed, returning his attention to the cheeseburger wrapper.

"And we put some new wheels on there, too," Terry adds, nodding to the larger black wheels resting horizontally along Bruiser's chest, alongside the pair of rollerblade wheels running vertically. Together, the wheels form a diamond, the black ones serving as the main source of movement while the rollerblade wheels stabilize him.

"This is awesome," Tammy agrees, turning to Terry. "This is just what he needed."

After being Cruiser-less for the past three days, Bruiser appears anxious to regain the mobility to which he's grown accustomed—perhaps a little too anxious.

As Terry and Tammy strap him in, we're hit with yet another wave of ripeness emanating from Bruiser's back end.

"What did you eat?" Tammy gasps, failing to remember the cheeseburger she'd fed him just minutes prior.

"Bruiser!" Terry cries, nearly abandoning his task altogether. "Come on, now!"

"Mercy!"

"Goodness!"

Bruiser, stone-faced, turns from Tammy to Terry and offers no indication of guilt.

Once the odor clears and the pair manages to strap him in, the three of us await Bruiser's grand return to the Cruiser.

"Well?" Tammy asks him. "What do you think?"

Bruiser takes a moment to settle in, remaining completely still.

"Give it a try," Terry says.

Sensing that Bruiser requires a bit of coaxing (and well aware that we are fresh out of cheeseburgers), Tammy resorts to the best motivation she has left at her disposal: herself.

Marching to the far side of the room, Tammy says, "Come on, I'm leaving."

Bruiser calls her bluff, turning his attention to me, then Terry.

"Bruiser, I mean it . . ." Tammy threatens, and though she doesn't mean it (there's not a force on earth strong enough to pry her away from her beloved dog), Bruiser suddenly feels the spirit soar within him. Like a spring set loose, he presses down hard with his front-left paw, propelling himself forward.

From my vantage point a few yards behind him, he resembles a linebacker tucked snug into his shoulder pads. He thunders through a doorway, then into a second room, squealing around a tight corner and circling back.

"Let's try it outside," Terry suggests.

Bruiser is only too happy to comply, and I watch, a bit shocked, as all sixty-five pounds of him blur toward the back door like a honey-colored lightning bolt.

The timid, backpedaling, gaseous dog I'd observed just minutes prior seems to have been replaced with a new dog, a confident dog, and God willing, a less gaseous dog as well. But most importantly, now he is a fully mobile dog, one who knows no bounds.

We open the back door and allow him to spill out into the sunshine. He's huffing, already exhausted by his lap around the workshop, and takes a moment to catch his breath.

"Come on, man, let's go," Tammy says, cajoling him across the asphalt lot. "Come on, buddy!"

Somewhere—well beyond the range of human ears—Bruiser hears a starter pistol. He takes off, tearing across the lot at speeds I haven't yet seen from him.

"Oh man, Traiden's got to see this," Terry laughs, slipping back inside to swap places with his partner. Moments later I glance to my left to see Traiden watching proudly as his star client squeals past.

"This is awesome," Traiden whispers.

Yet given what I know of Bruiser's extreme mobility issues, it's more than awesome; it's a borderline miracle.

Before anyone has a chance to become too sentimental, Bruiser transforms himself into a missile and fires.

"Bruiser, don't run into my car!" Traiden calls, but it's too late—the dog slams snout-first into its side paneling.

"Bruiser!" Tammy calls. "Come on, now. No using Traiden's car as a leaning post!"

But with no cheeseburger to dissuade him, Bruiser seems perfectly content to continue doing so—at least until Tammy marches over to redirect him, lifting him over the parking lot curb so he can try a bit off-roading. The combination of thick grass, dirt clods, and the occasional tree provides Bruiser an endless array of obstacles, though he hardly flinches, barreling through the terrain at top speed—at least until hitting a rut and rolling onto his back.

"Oooo!" Traiden and I moan. We half-cover our eyes, which only half keeps us from spotting Bruiser flopped upside down, his wheels still spinning in the air.

"We gotta get you a helmet, huh, Bruiser?" Traiden jokes.

Tammy doesn't laugh, doesn't even crack a smile. She is for Bruiser what Mickey was for Rocky—the never-say-die trainer who always pushes the contender to his limits.

"Come on," she barks, putting on her serious face, "you can do better'n that."

Never say can't, I think.

Proving his persistence, once he's turned upright, Bruiser readies himself for his second attempt at the troublesome rut.

"Come on," Tammy says. "What are you waiting for?"

Bruiser regains his composure, leans his head down, then presses his paw to the grass and shoots forward. He clears the rut in its entirety, hurtling a few inches into the air before landing safely on the other side. He squeals to a halt and the crowd goes wild, Traiden and me pumping our fists in the air like the pit crew for the winning car.

"Good work, Monkeyhead," Tammy says, revealing just a hint of a smile. "Way to show 'em how it's done."

NINE

.....

LETTING LUNA LEAD

Dogs are the leaders of the planet. If you see two life-forms,

one of them's making a poop, the other one's carrying

it for him, who would you assume is in charge?

—JERRY SEINFELD

A few weeks after meeting Kathie Schneider and Luna, I return once more to their doorstep. They're expecting me, and as Kathie pulls the door wide, she announces, "Well there's the famous author!" It's a title I hardly deserve, though after hearing a local radio interview in which I was featured, Kathie is kind enough to stroke Luna with one hand and my ego with the other.

"I'll just be a minute," Kathie says, turning toward the kitchen. "I'm going to slurp down this coffee. You can stay in here and interview Luna, get her side of the story."

If only I could, I think.

As I take a knee in Kathie's living room, offering Luna her obligatory belly rub, it's Kathie who shares the first story.

"We had a chipmunk in the house over the past few days," she tells me, making small talk as she takes a sip of coffee. "The first day I thought it was a bird in the basement, so I had a sighted friend come over, but of course it wouldn't make noise when somebody else was down there. So yesterday I heard it again, only this time it was a gnawing sound right outside the house."

"So what'd you do?" I ask.

"Well, I was pretty wild by that point, so I boiled water and threw it out the door where I thought I heard the noise. But," she sighs, "that didn't do anything either."

I smile.

"So finally, later that afternoon, when I heard scampering across my computer room floor, I thought, 'Oh shit, this is above and beyond here.' Luna came over — not exactly cringing, not shaking, but clearly concerned — and I thought, 'Well, if I'm hallucinating, at least she's got it too.'"

After enduring the mysterious creature's harassment awhile longer, Kathie eventually called upon neighbors to take care of the matter once and for all, sparing her from boiling and heaving any more water.

"My neighbor's wife spotted the chipmunk out of the corner of her eye," Kathie explains, "so she and her husband worked on him until they finally got him out."

"A live capture?" I ask while glancing down at Luna, now lost in her belly-rub bliss.

"Not even a capture," Kathie laughs. "They just sort of shooed him out."

Kathie gulps the last of her coffee, then redirects the conversation. "But enough about that," she says. "We have business to attend to."

First order of business: an autograph of Kathie's book, *To the Left of Inspiration*.

I've come prepared, toting a copy in the crook of my arm and a felt-tip pen in my hand. Though I'm hardly the famous author Kathie pegged me for, even I understand the autographing protocol — at least I think I do — though when I flip Kathie's book to the title page and extend the pen, I see that Kathie has little interest in what I have to offer. Instead, she takes hold of her book, bypasses the pen, and then presses a rubber stamp to an ink pad.

"The hard part is figuring out which side is up," she says, holding the stamp out to me. I adjust the rectangle in her hand, return it to her, then watch as she presses down firmly on the left side of the page.

"It pays to be a bureaucrat," she jokes, closing the ink pad.

"Not a bad technique," I admit, and one that I imagine could spare the John Grishams and Stephen Kings of the world more than a few unnecessary hand cramps.

When Kathie lifts the stamp, I examine her autograph more closely. There, alongside a stamped silhouette of a dog, is a pair of names: Kathie *and* Luna. It's the same sign-off I've noticed Kathie uses in her emails as well, and for me, this signals Kathie and Luna's inseparableness.

"Now then, on to the second order of business," Kathie says, leaving the kitchen and ushering us toward the front door.

Be positive, I think. *You can do this.*

A few weeks prior, when I'd first expressed interest in watching Luna lead, Kathie had been quick to welcome me on one of their walks, even going so far as to mention that I might be of some use.

"You can be my navigator," Kathie had said. "Help us learn the way to the new student center."

Though the jackhammers outside my office window had served as a constant reminder of our university's ongoing construction projects, I'd failed to consider how the construction might force Kathie and Luna to find alternatives to their usual routes.

I was happy to oblige, and grateful for the opportunity.

Summoning my inner Magellan, I watch as Kathie reaches for Luna's leash and harness, then snaps the gear into place.

As soon as the leash clicks into the harness, Luna transitions from off-duty house dog to on-duty Seeing Eye dog, revealing a part of her I hadn't yet observed. There are few visual clues to this transition aside from posture; Luna is no longer belly-up on the living room floor, but standing at attention just inches in front of Kathie.

"Your job," Kathie informs me as she reaches for the door, "is to stand a little bit off my right shoulder. When I need cueing or description I'll ask for it, and you'll get to figure out how to describe things in excruciating detail."

"Got it," I agree. "If my writing background has taught me anything, hopefully it's how to describe things in excruciating detail."

"Oh, you'd be surprised," Kathie smiles, closing the door behind us. "Anyway, we'll see. I just hope this is useful for you."

I have no doubt it will be. Though our first meeting offered me insight into how a Seeing Eye dog theoretically performs, I'm anxious to see Luna in practice as well. Further, I want to try to see how Kathie sees: to view the world stripped of one sense but augmented by an assistance animal.

We make it to the end of Kathie's walkway and turn left—in the exact opposite direction of the new student center.

I start to sweat, already beginning to feel a whole lot less positive.

Do I say something? I wonder. *Have I already failed in my role as navigator?*

"We're going by a particular route," Kathie explains, reading my mind.

Relieved, I listen closely as she talks me through the route she envisions for us; it's less direct, but requires only a single street crossing before leading us to a wooded trail that heads toward the student center's back entrance. She and Luna know the route generally, Kathie explains, but they need my help working out a few of the details along the way.

I like the idea of limiting street crossings, and even as Luna prepares to lead us across that one and only street along our route, I find myself growing nervous. I know she knows what to do, and even if she didn't, that I can serve as a safeguard. But my nervousness comes from realizing that when it's just Kathie and Luna—sans safeguard—their lives are dependent upon mutual trust. There are no backup plans, no fail-safes, no contingency for the wayward car whose wheels momentarily jump the curb. Certainly Kathie can hear traffic, and perhaps even sense it, but ultimately, Luna's eyesight and training make her the leader in the situation, even if she's the type of leader who knows how to take commands.

"Forward, girl," Kathie says, and after glancing behind her, Luna obeys, walking us the few dozen steps across the street and back onto the safety of the sidewalk.

It's an interaction Kathie and Luna negotiate on a daily basis, though I admit it's difficult for me to entrust my life to an animal — any animal — even one as highly trained as Luna. After observing one too many dogs indulge in the tasty treats found at the bottom of a litter box, I'd begun to question their judgment.

Of course, there's far more to dogs than the peculiarities of their palates, and when I consider also the tens of thousands of dogs who have improved the quality of life for tens of thousands of people, my trust in Luna grows. After all, Luna shows up for work and performs her task admirably every day of her life. Who among us can boast such a record?

As the three of us continue along the street — me fighting a few overgrown bushes on the right side of the sidewalk — Kathie and I run through all the usual topics: weather, work, current events.

What we don't talk about is what occurred on this very hill several years prior: how her previous Seeing Eye dog, a Labrador named Tatum, had spotted something on the opposite side of the street and jerked free from Kathie's grasp. How that dog had leapt headlong into traffic and was struck and killed by a car.

"The car didn't even stop," Kathie had confided in me during our previous conversation a few weeks prior. "I'm a divorced person, and I got to tell you, divorce is hard, but a death like that was harder."

But by the time we close in on the steps that will lead us down the wooded trail, all thoughts of death are left at a distance. Instead, we focus on the task at hand — one foot in front of the other — as Luna leads us toward the trail. As Kathie had previously assured me, Seeing Eye dogs aren't robots, which Luna proves as she begins tugging Kathie toward the most enticing smells.

"Come on, girl," Kathie says, redirecting Luna's attention to her task. "You can do it."

Luna *can* do it, and after Kathie's reminder, she leads us forward.

"Right when you can, Luna," Kathie says, anticipating the approaching trailhead. "Right when you can."

To me, she adds, "I think she likes me enough to show it to me."

It's a joke—at least I think so—though it raises an interesting question. Do Seeing Eye dogs—or any service animals for that matter—allow personal feelings to affect their work? Do they try harder when they love their human, or a little less hard when they don't? Surely service animals have been trained to perform their tasks without bias; nevertheless, they're not robots. They think, feel, and certainly have preferences (I return you to their cat-litter-loving palates).

Thankfully, for whatever reason—be it love, loyalty, or careful training—Luna spots the narrow opening between the trees and turns us right, leading Kathie and me down the wooden staircase.

As we start down the steps, I'm reminded of Kathie's earlier lesson—*be positive*. It's a lesson Kathie demonstrates now, offering Luna continual encouragement as we begin our descent.

"Good girl," Kathie says, holding tight to the handrail.

"Good girl," I parrot without thinking.

"Don't talk to her when she's working," Kathie reminds me, offering me a gentle prod to stay focused on my own task—not interrupting Luna's.

Stupid, I think. My praise was the result of my momentarily mistaking Luna for a pet when in fact she's a service animal. It's a minor trespass, though revealing nonetheless: proof that Luna doesn't need my praise the way a pet might; all she needs is for me to stay out of her way.

When we reach the bottom of the steps we're faced with two options: left or right.

Luna prefers left, a choice she makes clear by turning her body in that direction.

However, the student center is to the right, which is where Kathie needs her to lead us.

"The other way is a longer walk, yes, I understand that," Kathie says, trying to reason with her. "But we have places to go and things to do."

"And ice cream to eat," I add, clueing Luna in to the treat Kathie and I plan to reward ourselves with upon successfully reaching our destination.

Though I'm not sure the promise of ice cream tips the scales, eventually Luna relents. She leads us deeper into the woods, to a place where the traffic noise sinks to a murmur and is replaced by the sound of our feet (and paws) crunching against the mulch. Sunshine dapples the leaves, casting shadows along the path beneath us. It's a spectacular scene, and though Kathie doesn't experience it as I do, this hardly prohibits her from enjoying it fully.

"This is about as good as it gets," she smiles, tilting her head slightly back to catch the warmth of the sun on her face. She releases a contented sigh and then, upon hearing a jogger's shuffling feet just ahead of her, extends her joy outward.

"Good morning!" Kathie calls to the jogger.

"Hi!" the young woman says, a look of surprise crossing her face as the blind woman acknowledges her first.

"She could have said something," Kathie whispers to me once the jogger passes.

"Oh, she did," I assure her, thinking Kathie simply hadn't heard her. "She said hi."

"Yeah," Kathie says, "after *I* did."

It's a dilemma many face when interacting with people with special needs: confusing the disability with invisibility. I'll be the first to admit that at the conclusion of such an interaction, I'm often left replaying the scene in my head, wondering if I was sufficiently sensitive to the person's needs, or — equally awkward — if I was overly sensitive to the situation.

How, I wonder, *might I do a better job in the future?*

I'm not the only one whose fear of offending often proves offensive in itself. Kathie remarks that despite the time she has spent with professional colleagues at psychology conferences year after year, only on the most rare occasions do these colleagues offer to escort her from one panel to the next.

"Oftentimes these people are actually going to the exact place I'm going," Kathie says. "But people are shy. They don't want to offend."

"What would you prefer a sighted person do in that situation?" I ask.

"Just ask, 'How may I help?'" she tells me. "People can always refuse the help, but it doesn't hurt to ask."

It's advice I try to demonstrate throughout the remainder of our walk, piping up when I think I might be needed, but taking no offense when told I'm not.

As we head down the wooded trail, Kathie asks me to stay a bit farther behind her right shoulder.

"You're getting ahead of Luna," she explains, a trespass that risks undermining the dog's leadership.

I pause so Luna can catch up, taking advantage of my momentary stillness to peer up at the sun-drenched branches. The warmth feels wondrous on my skin, and as I wince at its brightness, I am reminded of Kathie's story of the moment she first realized she was blind. How, many years back, on a wondrous summer morning just like this, she and her brother had collected dandelions, though the weeds' yellow heads proved difficult for Kathie to distinguish amid the grays.

I ask her about this moment, about what it was like to be born sighted only to watch her eyesight fade at an early age.

"Well, my sight wasn't much to begin with," she explains as we walk, "so I didn't have far to go."

Nevertheless, she can still visualize the color of the dandelions in her mind's eye and, in fact, has about a first grader's "ten-crayon knowledge" of colors.

It's enough to allow her to imagine the green-leafed trees that surround us, as well as the yellow sun beating down on our shoulders.

Upon hearing another jogger shuffling past, Kathie calls out, "Good morning!"

The jogger waves instinctually—then spots Luna—and issues a verbal hello as well.

Satisfied with the interaction, Kathie smiles.

"Good job, Luna," she whispers, a line that falls naturally from her lips. "We're almost there."

∴

As we near the back entrance to the student center, it is I—not Luna—who am put to the test.

As we cross a footbridge leading us from the woods to the student center, Kathie asks, "If this is a clock and we're at six o'clock, where is the door?"

I grow nervous. Her question sounds suspiciously like a riddle, and I've always been terrible at riddles.

"Umm . . . it looks like twelve o'clock," I say, glancing up at the student center looming before us. "Straight ahead. Well . . . actually, there are sort of some trees up there, too," I begin second guessing myself, "so . . . maybe one o'clock? 1:30?"

"Okay, so where are we now?" she asks patiently.

"On a little sidewalk," I say.

"Okay," she repeats, "a little sidewalk with what on either side?"

"Uhhh . . . grass," I say, getting a sense of our location. "We're on a little sidewalk surrounded by grass."

"So if we overshoot it, I'm not going to be in the parking lot?"

"Correct," I say. "You'll be in the grass."

She nods, allowing the map of our location to materialize in her mind before she moves us forward.

"That's the kind of specific description I need," she explains. "I'm cueing you on how to cue me."

I nod, allowing humility to set in.

At the start of our walk, Kathie had cued me to cue her with "excruciating detail." Yet despite my best effort, I'd failed to do so.

Leading is hard, I realize, *especially when relying on verbal cues rather than the careful pull of a dog.*

Rather than use description to paint Kathie a carefully rendered visual portrait of our surroundings, all I'd done was offer her a general sense of the canvas.

Luna lifts her nose in the air as if catching a whiff of my incompetence. I take no offense. Though I have far fewer scent receptors than her, even I can smell it.

"Okay," I say, redoubling my efforts as we reach the middle of the parking lot. "Now keep heading straight maybe sixty feet or so, then we'll be at the door."

"In, in, in," Kathie says to Luna.

To me, she adds, "I try to cue her for success. So rather than 'Oh, whoops, Luna, you missed it,' I'm assuming she'll get it right."

She's being positive, I think.

And her positivity pays off.

Moments later we walk through the doors of the student center, at which point we're nearly blown back outside by the burst of air conditioning that greets us.

"Here," Kathie says, grabbing hold of my elbow, "I'll let you lead for a while."

Suddenly I become the Seeing Eye dog in the scenario, though perhaps I give myself too much credit by pretending I'm one of their pack. Nevertheless, I manage to direct us to the food court without any wrong turns, eventually bringing us to a halt before the glass cooler where the ice cream is displayed.

Just a few yards ahead of us, the woman working the cash register says, "The dog's being really good with all the smells."

Oh, this is no ordinary dog, I want to inform her, offering me a jumping-off point into a much longer lecture on the history of assistance animals from Dorothy Eustis to the present. But since I don't want to keep the ice cream waiting, I spare her the lecture.

"Thanks," I say simply, hoping my appreciation isn't construed as taking credit for Luna's fine behavior. After all, Luna is good because

Luna is Luna, though when I slide wide the cooler top, even our good dog lifts her nose to steal a quick sniff of what awaits us.

"Well, we've got plenty to choose from," I report to Kathie, listing off the many options available to us: "Klondike Bars, Ben and Jerry's, Choco Tacos, Reese's..."

"I think I'm going to do a Reese's," Kathie announces.

I retrieve it, followed by a Choco Taco for myself.

As I move toward the register, I remember my manners.

"Anything for Luna?" I ask.

"Is all the ice cream covered in chocolate?" Kathie asks.

"Uhh...pretty much," I say, taking one last look inside the cooler.

Eventually, we agree that Luna can have the last bite of my Choco Taco, as long as I'm careful to eat the chocolate parts myself. I assure Kathie that eating the chocolate parts won't be a problem for me; this is one task where I know I'll excel.

"Want to grab a few napkins?" Kathie suggests.

"Sure," I say, momentarily slipping my elbow from Kathie's grasp to retrieve them.

I know Kathie's in good paws; nonetheless, I take my momentary role as guide quite seriously, which means I sprint to the napkin dispenser and back with the speed of a number-one draft pick. Surely I look ridiculous, but I'm new at this, and since I've already screwed up on a couple occasions—praising Luna while she was on the job, as well as offering Kathie sub-par cueing—the last thing I want is to commit another sighted-person faux pas.

I return to my place beside Kathie, offer my elbow, and then lead us out the double doors toward a black table just beyond the shadow of the student center. The quad stretches before us, a mostly grass-less, straw-filled construction zone with a giant crane looming in the distance. Though it currently resembles a disaster area, by fall, I know the grass will have returned, along with trees and sidewalks—offering Luna plenty of new routes to learn.

Until then, we enjoy our ice cream amid the construction, unwrapping our respective treats and gobbling them down before they melt into puddles in our hands.

"You're a good cook," Kathie jokes through a mouthful of Reese's.

We whittle away the morning with chitchat, and when I finally glance down at what little remains of my Choco Taco, I realize I've whittled much of that away as well.

"Okay, I'm at final bite here," I announce, turning to Luna. "You ready for this, girl?"

I pick out the few chocolate flakes that remain, then hold the ice cream beneath the table just inches from Luna's nose.

Luna gives me her *Are you serious?* look, and after I assure her that I am—that she's more than earned this coveted last bite of Choco Taco—she devours it, no regrets.

We lock eyes, and the message is clear.

"You're welcome," I say, "thank you, too."

∴

As we prepare for our walk back to the house, Kathie returns to our earlier conversation about the chipmunk. How despite Luna's lack of vermin training, she still found a way to assist.

"When that chipmunk was in our space, Luna came right over to me," Kathie explains. "She was giving me information and seeking protection, I think, but it was a 'we're-in-this-together' feeling. She wasn't wearing her harness, so technically, she wasn't working, but she was definitely communicating."

I nod.

"As you saw with my cueing you during our walk, I need incidental information," Kathie explains. "That's what blind people need. And Luna's reactions to the chipmunk gave me all kinds of incidental information."

"A dog can show fear," I say, "and excitement . . ."

". . . and a cane can't," Kathie concludes.

As we head toward the edge of campus, we pass a crowd of forty or so middle-school-aged kids, all of whom shout while leaping atop one another's backs. They're having a great time, which is so obvious—even to Luna—that it appears as if it takes every bit of willpower that dog possesses to keep from pulling Kathie into the fray.

"Good job, Luna, good job. Luna, forward. Good job . . ." Kathie says, overwhelming her with praise.

Luna freezes, pitting the praise against the riotous fun occurring just ahead of her. She stares longingly at the children, then redirects the full power of her puppy-dog eyes directly in my direction.

I throw up my hands, making it clear to her there's no way I'm overruling Kathie. Not a chance.

"Good job, Luna, good job. Luna, forward. Good job . . ." Kathie repeats.

Eventually, Luna relents, rededicating herself to her task.

Of course, a cane would have offered no resistance, but no show of loyalty, either.

"I know, I know," Kathie sympathizes as we continue forward. "You would love to be part of that fun, wouldn't ya?"

Probably so, though judging by the care and attention Luna gives to each step, she seems to enjoy her work nearly as much as play.

Together, the three of us cross the street once more and head back toward the house. As we near it, we come within hearing distance of my two old friends—the frolicking neighbor dogs, who are once more engaged in serious play.

Focused on her task, Luna doesn't even bother looking up.

"Good dog, Luna, what a good dog," Kathie repeats.

She's absolutely, *positively* right.

TEN

.....

TRAVELS WITH SANDY

The dog is the only being that loves you

more than you love yourself.

—FRITZ VON UNRUH

A few weeks after chatting with Hartsdale Pet Cemetery director Ed Martin Jr., I'm back to thinking about Sandy, the droopy-eared Doberman with whom I shared my first seven years of life. Or rather, I'm back to thinking about what became of her. How after my mother, father, and I said our good-byes twenty-three years prior, her ashes were left to gather dust on the backroom bookshelf in our family home.

It's not that we'd stopped caring about her, but rather, that we cared so deeply we had no idea of how to say good-bye. And so we didn't. Not ever.

Yet after talking with Ed, I began to wonder if there might be some better way to honor our beloved dog, some way to finally give her the long-overdue burial she deserved.

"Let me get this straight," my wife, Meredith, said when I first broached the topic. "You want us to take a family vacation to a pet cemetery so you can bury some old dog?"

"Of course not," I laughed. "That makes it sound crazy."

She waited for my explanation.

"Well, pretty much what you said," I conceded.

To sweeten the deal (just in case driving a thousand miles with an eighteen-month-old to a pet cemetery wasn't enticing enough), I devised a full-fledged road trip, complete with stops in the Poconos and at Niagara Falls.

Meredith made clear to me that she would have much preferred a single stop at a beach — any beach — though she allowed me my indulgence.

"Thanks," I said. "I owe you one."

"Ten," she corrected. "You owe me ten."

∴

In late July, after my summer spent learning about people and their pets, our road trip begins with a stop at my parents' home in Indiana. We hadn't been back in months, though little appears to have changed. Little ever changes, including the sticker that has been prominently displayed on my parents' front door since I was a teenager, the one informing the Fort Wayne Fire Department of the many animals in need of saving should a fire occur. Over the years, as pets came and went, my mother remained dedicated to the task of scratching out the names of our departed pets and replacing them with the names of the new ones. Yet beneath her scribbles I can still make out the names of those pets now gone, each name serving as a time machine for some fast-fading era of my past.

Just what I need, I think as I glance the sticker on my way to the doorknob, *an existential crisis*.

Yet I can't blame the sticker alone. In truth, my parents' entire house is a time machine. This is the place where once, many years back, my mother arranged the wedding between our dog, Sydney, and our neighbor dog Dorsey. And it's also the place where we said our fond farewells to a cat, a couple of dogs, and herds of hamsters and gerbils too numerous to count. On the people side, it's the house where my brother and I grew up, the house where my mother grew up before us, and the house my grandparents built and lived in for nearly forty years before dying there as well.

As Meredith, Henry, and I enter the house, I realize that amid all these past memories are new memories in need of forming. My mother—queen of the scratched-out sticker—seems to realize this as well, though for her, no memory can ever be made on an empty stomach.

"How was your trip?" she cries, embracing all three of us. "What can I get you to eat?"

Ever since my first return home from college, I've come to expect this hero's welcome; my mother's elaborate meals (from crab legs to Cornish hens) have only grown grander since Henry's arrival on the scene. She views it as her grandmotherly duty to keep our kid plump, much as she's done for a generation of dogs.

As Mom begins her familiar clanging of pots and pans, I take to the living room, where I soon find that proof of my family's departed pets is hardly limited to the sticker on the door. In fact, our past pets' photos hang quite prominently along the walls. Not individual pet portraits, mind you, but family portraits that just so happen to include the pets. The most recent features our former dog Sydney, whose attire (Hawaiian lei) gives the impression that she's just stumbled into the frame after an evening at the luau.

Beyond the photos, perhaps the most tangible proof of my family's love for our pets is our backyard pet cemetery, which my father has faithfully tended for just shy of two decades. All but Sandy are buried there, an entire menagerie of animals long ago confined to blankets and boxes and marked with pieces of broken brick.

I hadn't been back there in years. Even if I'd wanted to, the promise of poison ivy and mosquito swarms made the trek all but unbearable. Add to these obstacles a quarter mile or so of overgrowth (not to mention a quicksand-ish mud pit) and my odds of completing the journey seemed just slightly better than summiting Mount Everest.

But if I don't do this now, I think, *I probably never will.*

"Hey," calls my twenty-five-year-old brother Brian, "welcome home." He's a filmmaker living in New Orleans, an adventurer, and judging by his willingness to return home to accompany us on our family trip to the pet cemetery, a glutton for punishment, too.

He hardly steps foot into the living room before I recruit him for my most recent spontaneous endeavor.

"Hey," I say, "did you happen to pack any old shoes?"

"Not really."

"That's okay," I shrug, "just be sure to keep an eye out for the mud pit."

We do keep an eye out for the mud pit. And the mosquitoes, and the poison ivy, and the tetanus we figure we'll likely acquire as a result of tromping in the forest armed with our father's rusty saws and pruning shears. After half an hour of sweat-dripping labor, we regress to the fort-building days of our youth, back when ripping through the wilderness in triple-digit temperatures was what we did for fun. We cut and hack our way back to the clearing, eventually catching our breath in the shade-filled cemetery at the edge of the property line.

"Huh, it's kind of nice back here," Brian admits.

"Peaceful," I agree.

He nods, then squats alongside the broken bricks to try to make sense of who's buried where.

"So is this Pumpkin or Sydney?" he asks, nodding to a dog-sized mound in the earth.

We aren't sure, and our attempt to find out becomes all the more difficult once we throw our former cat Morris into the mix.

"This one must be Sydney," I try, nodding to the third mound. "The dirt looks fresher, right?"

By process of elimination (as well as a bit more "eeny, meeny, miny, moe" than I'm comfortable admitting), we eventually settle on who's buried where, though our inability to identify the gravesites with any degree of accuracy is embarrassing—a fitting punishment, given our years of neglect.

How, I wonder, *have we grown so distant from these creatures we once held close?*

Hours after returning inside my parents' house, I try to make amends for our transgression, running my hands along the copper tin confined to the backroom bookshelf.

"Sorry, girl," I say, taking a peek at Sandy's ashes. "You deserve better."

And though I'm not quite sure where "better" is, I know it's out there somewhere.

∴

When we arrive in the Poconos two days later, I learn where better's not.

We've hardly pulled into the parking lot when a fellow guest steps forward to greet my parents, who had arrived a few minutes before us.

"This your first year here?" the guest asks.

"It is, actually," my mother says, expecting a warm welcome.

"Let me give you some advice," the guest says, turning serious. "Get in your car and drive away from here as fast as you can."

It's a joke (at least we think it is), though upon glancing at the rustic cabins and the children's splintering play area, I'm more than ready to take the man's advice.

The place resembles a summer camp gone to seed, a once-grand resort that over time has lost most of its grandeur. Nevertheless, the other guests—who I will later learn have been returning to this place with cult-like loyalty for decades—seem hardly to notice. They see the place only for the memories they've made there, and for them, every cobweb and loose nail commemorates some part of the shared story.

Over the next three days, as my family and I attempt to write our own story, I find—quite unexpectedly—that the place begins to grow on me. Not much, but enough to allow me a modicum of enjoyment as my dad, brother, a couple of cousins, and I dedicate long afternoons to cracking softballs deep into the fresh-cut grass while birds swoop overhead. When our arms begin to give, we take to the bows and

arrows, aiming for bull's-eyes we hardly expect to hit though occasionally do. We fish, embrace our inner shuffleboarders, even go for a dip
in the unheated outdoor pool. Though I'm not quite ready to join
the cult, I begin to understand the resort's appeal. This is a small slice
of land the world has left unblemished, an unknown mountainous
terrain that even the cell phone towers can't reach.

At night, as we fall asleep to owl hoots, Meredith and I joke that
the place has all the makings of a horror film.

"But in a good way," Meredith is sure to add.

On our second-to-last day—when we wake to find ourselves not
yet hacked to pieces—I grow even more nostalgic for this place we're
soon to leave.

Maybe a little too nostalgic.

Blame it on the birds, the butterflies, or the sunshine, but for whatever reason, prior to setting off on our last family hike, I excuse myself
to the cabin under the guise of retrieving some sunscreen. Instead, I
unzip my suitcase, remove the lid from the copper tin, and peer down
at Sandy's remains. Though I remember her as my well-built, brown-
furred friend, she looks like chalk dust now. I pour a few pinches of
her remains into a plastic film canister as I hear my family trudging
up the hill toward the cabin.

"Be right out!" I call, capping the canister and slipping it into my
pocket.

I step outside, smile, and keep my secret to myself.

"Now, then," I say, rubbing my hands together, "who here's ready
for a hike?"

∴

We hike past the ball field and the shuffleboard court before finding
our way onto a path running parallel to a stream. Henry's strapped
to my chest, babbling nonsense while squinting past the bill of his
floppy hat.

The trail breaks left toward the stream and we are immediately drawn toward it. A pair of cousins bound ahead while my wife, brother, father, and I linger just a few feet behind.

"You good?" Meredith calls as she starts toward the water.

"Sure," I say, "you go on ahead."

It's no beach, but she and I both know this stream is the closest she's going to get to one on this vacation.

As the others slip out of sight, I carry Henry along a flat rock at the edge of the stream. We peer down as the water gushes past, watching in silence as it cascades from one rock to the next with no sign of slowing. Overhead, the tree branches part, allowing the sun to peek through, and as it warms us in the wonder of the wild, I grip the film canister in my pocket, think, *Not a bad place to say good-bye.*

With my son pinned to my chest and my dog's ashes wearing a hole in my pocket, my existential crisis returns in full force. It's as if life and death have me by both ends, though if forced to choose, it's life I want to hold on to. Henry wraps an arm around my shoulder as I reach into my pocket for the canister. But just as I muster the courage to release Sandy into the wind once and for all, I hear a stick crack and, turning, spot my father ambling through the brush.

"Whatcha got there?" he asks.

I open my mouth to tell him, but he answers for me.

"That's her, isn't it?"

I nod guiltily.

A few days prior, when I first retuned to Indiana, I'd informed my father of my intention to say good-bye to Sandy for good. I'd told him about Hartsdale Pet Cemetery, about what a beautiful place it was, a near-perfect fit for our near-perfect dog.

It's an understatement to say he wasn't thrilled by the idea. He admitted that he, too, preferred having her ashes nearby, on a bookshelf perhaps, or at least buried in the backyard alongside all the rest. Why, he wondered, would we want to bury Sandy so far from her home?

After hearing him out, I began to get the sense it wasn't Sandy he grieved for, but the era she represented: the days when he himself was the young father and his loyal dog was *our* loyal dog.

True enough, I hadn't intended to release a portion of Sandy into some random stream in the Poconos, but I'd become momentarily overcome by the natural beauty of the place, realizing also that if I wanted to say good-bye for good, I might need the water's help.

My father clears his throat, rolls back his shoulders, and allows his eyes to refocus as he stares into the crystal-clear waters.

"Aww, geez," he says. "I'm going to get sad all of a sudden."

"Anything you want to say?" I ask.

We are all alone now, just a pair of fathers and sons in the woods.

"I will want to say something," he agrees. "Just . . . give me a second. I feel something coming."

I give him a second, then thirty, at which point we have regained the attention of my cousins, wife, and brother, all of whom watch solemnly at the impromptu ceremony occurring before them.

So much for not making a show of it, I think.

Finally, my father says, "You're a good dog, Sandy. And you'll be okay in this river."

It's a strange eulogy, though perhaps fitting given the strangeness of the situation. After all, what does one say when spreading the ashes of a dog so far gone? Yet what strikes me most about my father's speech isn't his words, but his tense.

"*You're* a good dog," he'd said.

You are.

Implying she still is.

As I open the canister and release Sandy's ashes into the stream, Henry begins babbling his own untranslatable eulogy. We don't understand a word of it, but it's as good as any other—something to fill our ears as the dust meets the water and rushes away.

Once the moment's over—once the others drift back into the woods—Brian stands alongside me and says, "What happened to the pet cemetery? I thought we were going to bury her there."

"I know," I agree, staring into the water. "So did I."

A few days later, we offer a second good-bye: this one to our cousins and our parents as we head toward Hartsdale, New York. Camera in tow, my brother joins Meredith, Henry, and me to serve as our private photographer for the remainder of the trip, boldly taking his place in the back of the van alongside the eighteen-month-old.

"You sure you can handle him?" I ask Brian as Henry leans forward in his car seat, shooting his sticky fingers toward the camera lens.

"Nope," Brian replies with a grin. "I'm not sure at all."

Two hours later, he's handling Henry better than most. Despite my premonitions to the contrary, his camera remains intact, and even more impressive, Henry appears to have momentarily silenced his seemingly endless vibrato.

Still, he's quite a squirmer, and we can't reach Hartsdale Pet Cemetery soon enough. I've barely unbuckled that boy from his car seat before he begins running toward the headstones.

"No desecrating graves!" I shout as he hurtles headlong down the paths. "I mean it!"

My wife gives chase, leaving me to my long-awaited moment to soak it all in as I step through the iron gates.

Cue the music and the close-up, I'm in heaven.

Ed wasn't exaggerating, I think as I peer out at the endless acres of carefully tended plots. *Not in the least.*

Though I've been in my fair share of cemeteries, I've never been in one as spectacular as this. The patch of land that was once Dr. Johnson's apple orchard is now covered with carefully preserved grave markers, many of which feature photos and names, as well as birth and death dates etched into stone.

In the cemetery's center is the caretaker's house—a one-story structure that currently serves as the cemetery's offices. I step inside and finally come face-to-face with cemetery director Ed Martin Jr., the boyish seventy-two-year-old whom, for the past few months, I've lassoed to his phone line so that I might better understand his business.

"Welcome to Hartsdale," he greets me. "How was the trip?"

I tell him it was great, that I'm excited to have finally arrived.

But what I don't tell him is that I'm also a bit nervous.

Though Ed and I had previously discussed the possibility of burying Sandy's remains in the cemetery, after my stream-serenaded moment in the Poconos, I'd begun to get cold feet. Part of my cold-footedness was related to cost—when all was said and done, a one-by-one-foot plot, including perpetual care, could run me around $1,400—though I was equally hesitant about the finality of burying Sandy so far from home. Perhaps my father's argument had resonated after all; perhaps there was comfort in knowing that some part of Sandy could always be found on the backroom bookshelf.

"I know it seems silly," I admit to Ed. "I mean, I came all this way, drove a thousand miles fully intending to bury her here, and yet . . . I'm not quite sure I'm ready . . ."

"Hey, no problem," Ed smiles. "Let me just run you through what you'd experience if you *did* bury here."

As we sit across from one another in the caretaker's house, he takes me through the procedure, treating me with the same respect he offers all those who intend to bury a pet in the cemetery. He begins with the paperwork, explaining that when you purchase a plot in this cemetery, you don't own the land, per se, but the exclusive right to bury an animal *on* the land.

But this "exclusive right" doesn't guarantee exclusivity forever, Ed adds. In order to retain the grave, a general maintenance fee must also be paid—a cost that runs around sixty dollars annually.

"And if the fee's not paid?" I ask.

"After four years, the pet owner loses the exclusive right to the land," he explains.

What this means, logistically, is that a groundskeeper must perform the uncomfortable duty of disinterring the pet, cremating it, and then scattering the ashes on the cemetery grounds, at which point the plot can be resold.

"We don't do this out of hard-heartedness, or to try to double the value of a plot," Ed assures, "but it's our job to protect the interests of all the pet owners who've buried here. It wouldn't be fair to you if you came back here to visit your pet in ten years and the grass was up to here," he says, motioning to his hip. "It's incumbent that everyone does their part to maintain the cemetery."

General maintenance fees vary, as do the prices of the plots themselves. The highest-priced real estate is often found along the footpaths, granting easy access to pet owners who plan to visit regularly.

"Come on," Ed says, standing from his chair, "let me show you around."

He leads me down the cemetery's many paths until we arrive at a small stone not far from the caretaker's house.

"People always ask me, 'What's the most unusual animal you've got buried here?'" Ed begins. "Well, here he is."

I kneel to get a better look at the marker, then smile as I recognize the name.

"Goldfleck," I whisper.

"The old lion," Ed confirms.

Through my research, I'd become quite familiar with the story of Goldfleck. How in 1908 Princess Elisabeth Vilma Lwoff-Parlaghy, the ex-wife of the Russian prince Lwoff, arrived in America alongside her entourage of pets (including a dog, a cat, an owl, an alligator, and a bear) and took up residence in Manhattan's Plaza Hotel. Though the hotel had already obliterated its pet policy to accommodate the princess, the staff were forced to stretch their accommodations further when she returned to the hotel one afternoon with a newly purchased lion cub trailing behind her.

"And the Plaza just let her keep a lion in her room?" I ask incredulously.

"Well, from what I can tell," Ed laughs, "she was pretty good at getting her way. Princesses have a knack for that."

Ed goes on to describe the funeral that followed soon after, how after Goldfleck's untimely death, the lion cub was brought to his final resting spot by way of horse-drawn wagon.

Ed continues his tour by leading me toward the gravesites of a few of the other more well-known animals, including Mariah Carey's cat as well as former New York Jets coach Allie Sherman's dogs.

"We've got a few like these," he admits, "but the majority of people who bury pets here are just normal, everyday people."

I nod.

"And occasionally," he adds, "these normal, everyday people end up really falling in love with this place themselves."

I think back to a previous phone conversation, one in which Ed had mentioned how humans sometimes request to have their ashes buried alongside their pets. Initially, I'd thought the practice strange, though I'd forgotten all about it until Ed begins pointing out their graves.

"This site belongs to Marjorie and Arthur," Ed says, nodding to the stone. "They share it with their cats."

Ed explains how, following his wife's death, Arthur came to the cemetery seeking a final resting place for his wife and their pets.

"His wife had been cremated," Ed explains, "and though not all of their cats were dead yet, at least half of them were. All their ashes were together in the house, and Arthur was afraid that after he died someone might come in, clean out the house, and toss both his wife's and their cats' remains. So he bought this plot," Ed says, "to try and avoid that situation."

"Well, that doesn't sound so strange," I admit. "Just practical, really."

"It isn't strange," Ed agrees, "at least not to me."

As if to prove it, he leads me to the shadiest spot in the cemetery.

"Where are we now?" I ask.

"This," he smiles, "is the Martin family plot."

"Right here?" I ask. "Right where we're standing?"

He nods.

"I still have some work to do," he adds, kicking at a few weeds that have cropped up around the headstones, "but this is us. These are my folks, and these are my wife's folks, and guess who these will be for?" he laughs, nodding to a few unetched marble slabs alongside the others.

In the space just ahead of the grave markers is a marker for the

Martin family's most recent dog, a shepherd-Lab mix named Coach. To the right of Coach are two smaller, more curious graves.

"Hamsters?" I ask quite seriously.

"My grandkid's fish," he corrects.

There's something revealing about a man content with being buried alongside a couple of fish. The decision seems ego-less, one free of species-related hierarchies. Immediately, my mind travels to ancient Peru, to the Chiribaya people's decision to bury their humans alongside their dogs, granting equal respect to both.

Yet while the Chiribayas did it, as well as the Phoenicians in Ashkelon, Ed admits that even today—thousands of years later—pet burials aren't for everyone.

"We bury about 425 pets a year here," he says, "and the number of pets that annually pass away in the metropolitan area is somewhere around 50,000."

Nevertheless, for the small percentage of folks who do decide to bury their pets with all the accouterments generally reserved for humans, Hartsdale serves as a perfect fit.

"When I talk to the folks who actually dig the graves, I always say, 'You don't have to *believe* in this whole thing, but you have to *understand* it. The bottom line is, you have to respect it.'"

I nod and he continues.

"I tell them that their job is more than just digging a hole, putting a pet in a casket and burying it. I tell them that what we're 'selling'—and I hate to use that term—is a way to make people feel a bit better than when they walked in here."

It's a way to help others, I think, *any way we can.*

In my own effort to help Ed, I allow our conversation to wind down so that he might get back to helping others. Though before I say good-bye, I mention the film canister in my pocket.

"I don't think I'm ready to bury all of Sandy," I say, "but do you think it'd be okay if I left a part of her here?"

He points me toward the memorial garden, not far from the crematorium.

As I start down the hill toward the garden, Ed calls out to me.

"Hey," he says.

I turn.

"What got you started on this project anyway? Was it your personal pet?"

I explain that Cici, though just middle-aged, certainly played some role in my interest, though so did my recent foray into the world of parenthood. I nod to Henry, who by this point has grown tired of the cemetery and returned to his vibrato as he bumbles down the paths.

"I guess I've just been thinking about mortality a lot lately," I shrug.

Ed nods, shooting a quick glance toward the Martin family plot just a hundred or so yards away.

"I wish you luck with your project," he says.

As Ed returns to the caretaker's house, I turn my attention in the opposite direction, toward Henry, whose wails sound as sharp as a dog whistle. I jog to retrieve him, though as I do, I hear additional sobbing coming from somewhere farther down the hill. I turn my head toward the sound to spot a man in dress pants and a button-down shirt kneeling before a grave. He's accompanied by a pair of friends, both of whom stand like sentinels on either side of him.

Though Ed informed me that these sorts of dramatic occurrences were rare in the cemetery, they weren't without precedent. After all, losing a loved one — regardless of species — still means losing a loved one. Sometimes grief is expressed privately, sometimes publically, and as Mrs. M. F. Walsh seemed to have proved by way of her pets' mausoleum, it's sometimes expressed extravagantly as well. Throughout his years at Hartsdale, Ed has come to understand that there is no wrong way to grieve. Sure, some expressions of grief may seem more culturally acceptable than others, but cultural acceptance hardly translates into a more effective grieving process. Grief, after all, cannot be streamlined, multitasked, or micromanaged. And in my own experience, treating it like an ailment only leads one further from the cure.

I shoot the crying man a sympathetic look before attempting to deal with my own crying boy. Meredith, Brian, and I eventually corner him near the memorial garden at the bottom of the hill.

He searches for an escape route, but finding none, bursts into a second round of tears.

"Calm down, boy," I joke. "The ceremony hasn't even started yet."

Once his crying subsides, the four of us gather round the garden's wood-carved lamb, lion, and various other animals, all of which appear to be living in perfect harmony. It's hard to know just how many pets' ashes have been spread here before, though I'm prepared to add one more to the count. I reach into my pocket for the film canister and hold tight to a small portion of Sandy's ashes.

"Well," I ask, "anyone have anything to say for Sandy?"

I glance around, but since my wife and son never knew her, and my brother has only the foggiest memory of her, I alone am left to give the eulogy.

Inspired by the sound of a truck groaning somewhere in the distance, I think back to the day Sandy's foot was run over by a UPS truck, and how as a result, she spent the rest of her life barking at every UPS truck that ever dared pass our house. As a young boy, I'd knelt beside her as we stared out the window, barking at every damn truck in their fleet.

I smile as I uncap the canister, allowing her ashes to mix with all the others in the memorial garden.

"Well, Sandy," I say, "I sure hope you're giving the UPS trucks plenty of hell up there in heaven."

The ashes vanish, and as I slip the canister back into my pocket, I turn to find Henry already stumbling back toward the van.

"Okay, then," I sigh, a half-smile lingering across my face. "I guess it's time to move on."

∵

And move on we do, to our final stop: Niagara Falls—a seemingly fitting end to our journey. We're beat—dog-tired, if you will—and after clocking a thousand-plus miles on the odometer, the most we feel like doing is kicking back and soaking-in the falls' panoramic views.

Though I don't regret our high-intensity vacation (at least not publically), I admit to beginning to better understand the perks of sipping a mai tai on the beach.

Still, when we arrive at Niagara Falls State Park—no mai tais in sight—we try to make the most of it. It's early morning, but already the park is claustrophobically crowded, overrun with thousands of flip-flopped tourists, most of whom appear in equally desperate need of mai tais. I can't help but notice that a collective sense of exhaustion seems to permeate throughout.

"Is it just me," I ask Meredith, "or does even the waterfall appear a bit sluggish?"

As I lock eyes with the other droopy-eyed parents, we all seem to acknowledge our one shared miscalculation: while road trips sound wonderful in theory, when put into practice, they threaten even the most well-adjusted among us. There, in the asphalt prisons better known as highways, families forced to endure too many turnpikes and too few bathroom breaks often make for a deadly combination. Nevertheless, my fellow droopy-eyed parents and I remain firm in our refusal to admit our miscalculation to our children. Instead, we follow another script, one that reads, *Though we may have lost our tempers, our wallets, and our sanity, we are here. And come hell or high water, we're going to have a damn good time.*

"Are we having fun yet?" I ask miserably as I surrender ten bucks to a parking meter, then crawl forward at a snail's pace while a gaggle of disinterested teenagers text one another without bothering to notice the natural wonder roaring before them.

"Great. Keep texting," I grumble as the bow-headed parade continues. "Don't let that waterfall distract you."

We find a parking spot, eventually, and then march through the turnstiles and into the carnival-like atmosphere that awaits us.

We have plans to do it all—our break-the-bank, once-in-a-lifetime adventure, complete with excursions to the aquarium, the Gorge museum, the Cave of the Winds tour, and, of course, a ride on the legendary *Maid of the Mist*. I part with my credit card, wincing as the woman behind the register charges me a princely sum and demands I have a nice day.

"I'll try," I promise, packing myself sardine-style into the trolley car that awaits us.

I've hardly joined the herd when I'm suddenly paralyzed by a blast of body odor, one that seems greatly at odds with the natural splendor I've paid good money to see. Breathing from my mouth, I stare longingly out the window, trying hard to dream up an exit strategy that doesn't involve a waterfall and a barrel.

My pity party's in full swing, at least until I begin eavesdropping on the conversation between two strangers seated directly ahead of me. A glance forward reveals them to be a couple of red-blooded Americans, thick-necked and jowly. They're the kind of guys I can easily envision high-fiving one another when the right team scores a touchdown, guys whose primary forms of affection involve head-locks and noogies. But in this moment, as the trolley transports the whole horde of us from one attraction to another, the jowly men's testosterone seems to have leveled. From what I overhear, they're fresh from seeing the falls and, judging by their conversation, have clearly been affected by it.

"I didn't know what the big deal was about a bunch of water," the first man admits, "but I get it now."

"Hell yeah," the second man agrees. "That's a *lot* of water, after all."

I try to keep from rolling my eyes at their less-than-astute observations.

"But I'll tell you one thing," the first man says, his thick New York accent growing more pronounced with every word. "This here is what it's all about. Being able to share this sort of thing with your family."

Ironically, he's not sharing it with family, but instead is cramped in a too-tight trolley-car seat alongside a stranger. From what I can gather, both their families appear to be seated several rows ahead, their children flicking one another's earlobes while their wives wearily issue empty threats of groundings soon to come.

"Man, I hear that," the second man agrees. "This *is* what it's all about. Everything else is just dust."

Suddenly, I'm no longer rolling my eyes. I wouldn't dare.

Dust, I think, reaching a hand into my pocket to touch the film canister still there. *Everything else is just dust.*

∵

We disembark from the trolley and — after half a dozen "excuse mes" and "pardon mes" — we arrive at the docking site of the lordly *Maid of the Mist.* For over 150 years, the boats have taken visitors as close to the falls as safely possible, cramming hundreds of poncho-clad patrons onto both decks of the eighty-foot vessels, all of which are left bucking in the swirl of Niagara's waters.

Meredith, Brian, and I slip into our ponchos, but when I try to fit Henry into his, he refuses. Vehemently.

"Come on, boy," I say, trying to reason with him. "You're going to love this. We're going to see water."

"Wawa!" he wails, contributing a few gallons more with his tears.

"Wawa," I agree, rolling the poncho to attempt a quick strike to slip it over his head. "We're going to see wawa."

My promise of wawa has little effect, and by this point, as he collapses to the damp cement, wailing and poncho-less, we begin drawing the ire of other visitors trying to have their own damn good time.

Take a picture, I think, *it'll last longer.*

After a bit more maneuvering, I eventually poncho Henry into submission, though he's not happy about it, which means none of us are particularly happy about it, either. Thankfully, the American falls provide us just enough decibels of deafening roar to drone out most of the wails.

"Wawa," I repeat as we board the boat. "Just calm down and look."

Eventually he does, and when he actually sees the watery wonder stretched before us, the wailing suddenly stops.

"See?" I say as we take our place next to Brian and Meredith along the port-side railing. "This isn't so bad."

Once the wailing stops, we all take to our cameras, yet despite our combined efforts, neither my brother (the professional) nor Meredith and I (the amateurs) can seem to snap enough pictures to sate us. As I glance up from my viewfinder, I see that we're far from the only shutterbugs aboard this boat. It's as if every last passenger has suddenly become entranced by the falls, each of us trying to preserve the moment while mostly missing it, instead. It's a mistake I know well: placing too much emphasis on what comes next and not enough on now.

For more than two decades, I'd tried to preserve Sandy by letting her sit dormant on a backroom bookshelf. Nobody ever thanked me. Nor should they have. After all, abandoning her there wasn't so much a means of saying good-bye as a means to keep from doing so. My family and I left her there, waiting for the day when saying good-bye to her might feel right. What we failed to realize, however, is that saying good-bye to a pet rarely feels right. It almost always just feels terrible.

It has taken me twenty-three years—well over one hundred dog years—to come to terms with this realization. In all that time, I'd been using Sandy's copper tin as my crutch, convincing myself that my ability to remember her was somehow tied to her ashes.

My trolley-car sages had informed me otherwise, helped me understand that Sandy's ashes were just ashes, her dust just dust, and what matters most is the here and now.

These are the thoughts that wash over me as the boat leaves the dock and barrels forth, catching us in a spray of mist and water and coating our blue ponchos in droplets. I glance over as Henry rests comfortably against his mother's hip, gesticulating toward the falls with the confidence of a well-seasoned tour guide.

In a moment of inspiration—as we rock back and forth amid the maelstrom of Canada's Horseshoe Falls—I excuse myself past a hundred clicking cameras and take my place on the starboard side of the boat. There, supported by the crushing crowds of strangers on either side of me, I reach quickly into my pocket.

As the moment begins hurtling toward history, I reach frantically for the film canister. I flick the cap off one last time and scatter Sandy's ashes into the blue-and-gray swirl just beneath me. For an instant, her ashes cling to the air before merging with the timeless waters and disappearing for good. I am left breathless, soaking, and trembling beneath my poncho.

I close my eyes, trying hard to remember what it once felt like to be Sandy's boy, to be some young kid who'd loved his dog terribly, or wonderfully, or both.

When I reopen my eyes, I find myself facing the approaching American shore. I glance around to notice that the camera-clicking tourists have at last given their trigger fingers a rest. We have all seen what we have come to see, done what we have come to do.

Yet despite saying good-bye to Sandy on three separate occasions—in the Poconos, and in Hartsdale Pet Cemetery, and even at Niagara Falls—I still find myself feeling much the same as before. I cannot overstate the anticlimax of it all. Though I understand grief is a process, I always figured an epic road trip—complete with ash-scattering stops both planned and spontaneous—would surely lead this process to its end.

But as the boat rocks beneath my feet, I feel no closure, just the continued unsteadiness of the water.

I seek solace alongside my family on the port side. I wipe the mist from my eyes with my poncho, then press a hand to Henry's small back.

He turns from the falls to momentarily stare at his hard-hearted father.

"Wawa," he says at last, pointing me back toward the shore.

"Dust," I correct. "That's just dust."

∴

Four hundred and fifteen miles later, the minivan shudders to a halt in my parents' drive. I remove the key from the ignition, promising myself not to reinsert it until I absolutely have to. We have driven too far, seen too much, and as our vacation winds down, I begin to feel in desperate need of a vacation.

Nevertheless, I take some pride in knowing that we have survived the trip—survival being the best possible outcome given the death march I'd put us through. Meredith, Brian, and Henry are happy because the trip has at last reached its end, and I'm happy because I've at last said good-bye to my dog.

Well, sort of kind of happy.

When I return what's left of Sandy's remains to the backroom bookshelf, I can't help but feel the same lingering doubt I'd felt aboard the *Maid of the Mist* a few days prior. My piecemeal approach to saying good-bye had lacked something. Though I've had 415 miles to figure out what that "something" is, the answer still eludes me.

Perhaps you can't force closure, I decide as I continue unloading the minivan. *Maybe I've been barking up the wrong tree all along.*

Suddenly my eyes veer to the right tree—or trees—that lead to our backyard pet cemetery.

It's the trail my brother and I had hacked our way through the previous week, though I now wonder if all our spontaneous trail clearing had prophesized the one place Sandy truly belonged.

I hurl the last of the luggage into the house, then reach for my brother.

"Come on," I say, "I think we've got to make one last stop."

Exhausted and bedraggled as we are, we still find the gusto to take once more to the woods, to the pet cemetery, to lay our dog to rest. But before we do, we grab our supplies: a shovel, a film canister of ashes, and my grandparents' copy of *The Union Prayer Book for Jewish Worship*. Serendipitously, I flip it open to the one dog-eared page in the book, which just so happens to be titled "Prayer in the Cemetery: Dedicating a Tombstone."

"Well, that was a little too good to be true," Brian says, "but . . . are we sure Sandy's Jewish?"

Straight-faced, we look at one another before the absurdity of our situation becomes clear to us.

"You know, I'm not sure if Sandy was Jewish or not," I smile. "Somehow that never came up."

Since we don't have much in the way of a tombstone, I grab a fist-sized broken brick and decide it'll have to do. And then, to round out the ceremony, Brian and I leash the pair of dogs currently in the house, my parents' dog, Rocky, as well as my own mutt, Cici.

"If people could see us now," I say as we weave through the trees, a shovel in one hand and a Jewish book of prayer in the other. I'm nervous, but excited as well, as are Rocky and Cici, who lead us through the brambles as if knowing the way by heart.

We bypass the gerbil and guinea pig graves, eventually arriving at the section of cemetery reserved exclusively for dogs and cats.

"Here we are," I say. "Sandy's *final*, final resting place."

Then, much as our father had many times before, Brian grabs the shovel and places a heel atop the blade. He presses down hard, moving the first inch of dirt, then tossing it to the side. He repeats the process while the dogs watch on, panting and entangling their leashes around the branches.

After several more minutes of digging, Brian peers down into his eight-by-eight-inch hole. It's a good-sized grave—more than sufficient for the film canister of ashes. We take a moment to soak it all in, just Brian and me and a pair of dogs searching for a bit of backyard solemnity. But upon glancing around, I realize that there are far more than a pair of dogs alongside us. Our former dogs Pumpkin and Sydney are here, too, and Morris the cat, not to mention the multitude of others we loved and lost throughout our youth. By this logic, Sandy's funeral is well attended, by a whole host of creatures that knew the Hollars family well before leaving.

Though my rabbinical training is limited, I flip to the dog-eared page of the Jewish book of prayer with the expertise of a newly bar mitzvahed thirteen-year-old.

"Okay, here we go," I say, clearing my throat and placing a finger to the pages:

"In Thine unsearchable wisdom Thou has taken our dear Sandy from us," I read, filling in the name as indicated. "But the deep and tender love which attached us unto our Sandy is strong as death. Striving to soothe the sorrow of our hearts, we dedicate this stone to-day."

I place the film canister into the ground, watch as Brian tamps the soil back into the earth.

We're unsure what to do next, so I take my cue from the other graves — placing the broken brick atop the freshly dug mound.

"Well," I say, "I guess that does it."

"Yup," Brian agrees.

Though the anticlimactic feeling remains, I'm beginning to feel more comfortable with it. After all, if enduring a loved one's death is the climax, what more can we expect from what follows?

In truth, I'm not sure what I expected — a miracle, I suppose. A parted sea or burning bush or some other confirmation that at last what I'd done was right. But the God I know rarely speaks with such booming-voiced clarity, and never to tell me I'm right. Rather, he seems to like to keep me guessing, forcing me to mull over my choices in the hope that free will might guide me.

But as Brian and I learn as we head back toward the house, sometimes free will serves as a faulty navigator.

"Where are we?" I ask, scanning the wilderness that surrounds us. "How in the world did we get lost in our own backyard woods?"

Though our backyard "woods" can't be more than a couple of acres, it's so densely packed that a couple of acres is all it takes to get us lost. We blink, and somehow the bramble thickens around us, ensnaring us in thorns and thistles. I snap branches, dodge poison ivy, and try to keep from smacking Brian in the face with a wayward limb. Despite our discomfort, the dogs appear to be thoroughly enjoying themselves, as if all their tugging was part of some master plan to keep us (and them) in the woods awhile longer.

As the mosquitoes begin to swarm, Cici and I pop out of the woods and into the knee-deep grass surrounding an overgrown tennis court. I haven't been there in years, though when I was younger, my grandfather would lead me by the hand to this very place, helping me down the wooden steps into the sunken court that belonged to his neighbor. Back then, the place had seemed a secret wonderland, though now, so many years later, the wonder has been left to ruin alongside the paint-chipped court.

"Where are you?" my brother shouts from the edge of the woods.

"Tennis court," I holler back.

Rocky pulls him into the high grass, returning him to this forgotten place, one still haunted by the memory of our grandfather thwocking tennis balls at us from his place across the wilted net.

In the film version, this is the moment my life begins flashing before my eyes — quick cuts of Sandy and me frolicking alongside a lake, followed by my grandfather feeding me tennis balls, then my brother and me taking turns blowing out birthday candles.

You get the picture. You know the scene. Probably, you've lived it yourself.

Achy, tired, and batting at the swarms of flies still hovering around our heads, Brian and I take one last look at the court before allowing the dogs to drag us to the safety of our parents' backyard. Though the dogs opt for the squirrel-chasing circuitous route, we eventually spot my mother watering the backyard plants.

"There you guys are," she calls out to us. "Are you hungry?"

As my brother retreats to the house to scrub the poison ivy away, I distract my mother from her urge to whip up a feast by asking for her help in washing the dogs. They're filthy and bur-riddled, their black coats seeming to have absorbed a wide array of backyard flora.

Mom's happy to help, and soon we're both running our hands through the dogs' thick fur, lathering them in soap, then holding tight to their leashes as we spray them clean with the hose. At first the dogs shy away from the water, though once our task is complete and they've been upgraded from "filthy" to "slightly less filthy," they take to zooming around the backyard, thrilled by their newly cooled bodies. The hose water serves as their Fountain of Youth, returning them to a puppy-like state. They run joyously, unstoppably, even take to barrel rolling when the time is right. They snap at butterflies, chase a few more squirrels, and bark at every last cloud in the sky.

I want to join them, run and snap and chase and bark myself. Want to howl at the moon, too, transform myself into some happy night-time howler just like Dorsey.

"You guys have fun out there?" Mom asks me as we watch them run, though sensing she's said the wrong thing, rephrases: "I mean, did it go okay with Sandy?"

"Yeah," I say. "I think it went okay."

What I don't tell her is how even twenty-three years after Sandy's death, that dog still had a lesson to teach me. No, she didn't teach me to live life with hope or to keep from judging books by their covers. Nor did she teach me about resilience, or staying positive, or helping others any way I could.

Though Sandy's lesson had sat dormant for years—left to percolate in a copper tin on a backroom bookshelf—when I was finally ready to hear it, she said it loud and clear.

Quite unexpectedly, that old dog of mine had taught me a new trick:

While we grieving pet owners often feel all alone, we are all alone together.

SOURCES

This account was written using various sources, including firsthand accounts, scholarly research, and online and newspaper articles. What follows is a list of the sources I most heavily replied upon while crafting individual chapters. The sources are listed in approximate chronological order according to the information's placement within each chapter. If a source was employed multiple times throughout a chapter, I listed it only upon its initial use.

PROLOGUE
The introduction was written with support of the following sources: Stager, "Why Were Hundreds of Dogs Buried at Ashkelon?"; Atwood, "Peru's Mummy Dogs"; Miller, "Attitudes toward Dogs in Ancient Israel"; American Pet Products Association, "Pet Industry Market Size and Ownership Statistics"; "2012 United States Federal Budget," *Wikipedia*; "Top Dogs in Pet Cemeteries," *USA Today*.

1. SNIFFING FOR TROUBLE
The first chapter was written with support of the following sources: interview with Bekah Weitz, June 13, 2013; interview with Amber Gooden; Humane Society of the United States, "Animal Cruelty Facts and Statistics"; Kellert and Felthous, "Childhood Cruelty toward Animals"; Brantley, "FBI Perspective on Animal Cruelty"; Luke, Arluke, and Levin, *Cruelty to Animals and Other Crimes*; Ascione

et al., "Battered Pets and Domestic Violence"; Ascione, Weber, and Wood, "Abuse of Animals and Domestic Violence"; Recruiter.com, "Salary for Animal Control Workers"; Bartram and Baldwin, "Veterinary Surgeons and Suicides"; Watkins, "Paper Delves into British Veterinarians' High Suicide Risk"; O'Rourke, "High Suicide Risk for British Veterinarians"; Platt et al., "Suicidality in the Veterinary Profession"; DeGioia and Lau, "Veterinarians Prone to Suicide."

2. OLD DOGS, NEW SHTICKS

The second chapter was written with support of the following sources: interview with Amy Quella, May 24, 2013; Muttville Senior Dog Rescue, "Awards and Accomplishments"; Maddie's Fund, "Sherri Franklin"; American Pet Products Association, "Pet Industry Market Size and Ownership Statistics"; Eau Claire County Humane Association, "Cost of Pet Ownership"; Weeks, "Recession and Pets"; Senior Dog Project, "Top Ten Reasons to Adopt an Older Dog"; Robinson and Segal, "Therapeutic and Health Benefits of Pets"; Knight and Edwards, "In the Company of Wolves"; United Cerebral Palsy of Philadelphia and Vicinity, "Benefits of Pet Therapy"; Nazario, "27 Ways Pets Can Improve Your Health."

3. CRUISIN' FOR A BRUISER

The third chapter was written with support of the following sources: interview with Tammy and Ken Gurklis, June 23, 2013; O'Brien, "Chippewa Valley Experts Help Animals"; Sayre, "Wild World of Animal Prostheses"; American Society for the Prevention of Cruelty to Animals, "Puppy Mill FAQ"; Humane Society of the United States, "Puppy Mills"; Animal Welfare Act, *Animal Welfare Information Center*; Parham, "Remarks"; Animal Rescue Corp., "What Is a Puppy Mill?"; "Dogs That Changed the World," *Nature*.

4. FOLLOW THE LEADER

The fourth chapter was written with support of the following sources: interview with Katherine Schneider, June 17, 2013; Schneider, *To the*

Left of Inspiration; Ostermeier, "History of Guide Dog Use by Veterans"; Eustis, "Seeing Eye"; Seeing Eye, "Mission, Vision and Goals"; Seeing Eye, "Frequently Asked Questions"; Seeing Eye, "Our Mission & History"; Skloot, "Creature Comforts."

5. I LEFT MY HEART IN HARTSDALE

The fifth chapter was written with support of the following sources: Martin, *Dr. Johnson's Apple Orchard*; Martin, *Peaceable Kingdom in Hartsdale*; interview with Mary Thurston; American Society for the Prevention of Cruelty to Animals, "What to Do If Your Pet Has Died at Home"; interviews with Ed Martin Jr., May 8 and 23, 2013; "Top Dogs in Pet Cemeteries," *USA Today*; Thurston, National Register for Historic Places application.

6. APOLLO'S DEED

The sixth chapter was written with support of the following sources: interview with Bekah Weitz, August 6–7, 2013; interview with Sara Stary, August 6–7, 2013; Eau Claire Police Department Incident Report; Eau Claire Police Department Voluntary Witness Statements; *Beyond the Myth*; You, "Two Dogs Attack Pet Cat"; Eau Claire County Humane Association, "Animal Statistics 2012–2009"; Human Society of the United States, "Pet Overpopulation"; "NC Shelter Kills 99% of Animals," WRAL.com; interview with Scott and Sally Dawson.

7. BINGO WAS HER NAME

The seventh chapter was written with support of the following sources: interview with Emily Townsend; interview with Nikki Ristau, August 15, 2013; interview with Amy Quella, August 15, 2013.

8. THE BIONIC DOG

The eighth chapter was written with support of the following sources: interview with Terry Kufner; interview with Traiden Oleson; interview with Bob and Elsbeth Johnson; interview with Tammy Gurklis, July 15, 2013.

9. LETTING LUNA LEAD

The ninth chapter was written with support of the following sources: interview with Katherine Schneider, July 10, 2013; Schneider, *To the Left of Inspiration.*

10. TRAVELS WITH SANDY

The tenth chapter was written with support of the following sources: interview with Ed Martin Jr., July 27, 2013; Martin, *Peaceable Kingdom in Hartsdale.*

BIBLIOGRAPHY

INTERVIEWS

Dawson, Scott and Sally. Personal interview. August 10, 2013.

Gooden, Amber. Personal interview. June 13, 2013.

Gurklis, Tammy. Personal interview. July 15, 2013.

Gurklis, Tammy and Ken. Personal interviews. June 23, August 16–18, 2013.

Johnson, Bob and Elsbeth. Personal interview. July 8, 15, 2013.

Kufner, Terry. Personal interview. July 8, 15, 2013.

Martin, Ed, Jr. Telephone interviews. May 8, 23, July 27, 2013.

Oleson, Traiden. Personal interview. July 8, 15, 2013.

Quella, Amy. Personal interviews. May 24, August 15, 2013.

Ristau, Nikki. Personal interviews. May 24, August 15, 2013.

Schneider, Katherine. Personal interviews. June 17, July 10, 2013.

Stary, Sara. Personal interviews. August 6–7, 2013.

Thurston, Mary. Personal interview. May 22, 2013.

Townsend, Emily. Personal interview. August 15, 2013.

Weitz, Bekah. Personal interviews. June 13, August 6–7, 2013.

OTHER SOURCES

American Pet Products Association. "Pet Industry Market Size and Ownership Statistics." 2012. Web. June 30, 2013.

American Society for the Prevention of Cruelty to Animals (ASPCA). "Puppy Mill FAQ." 2015. Web. January 2015.

———. "What to Do If Your Pet Has Died at Home." 2013. Web. December 2013.

Animal Rescue Corp. "What Is a Puppy Mill?" *Puppy Mills*. Web. September 14, 2013.

Animal Welfare Act. *Animal Welfare Information Center*. U.S. Department of Agriculture, National Agricultural Library. Web. August 9, 2014.

Antelyes, Jacob. "When Pet Animals Die." *Pet Loss and Human Bereavement*. Ed. William Kay et al. Ames: Iowa State University Press, 1986. 37–41. Print.

Ascione, Frank, et al. "Battered Pets and Domestic Violence." *Violence against Women* 13.4 (2007): 354–73. Print.

Ascione, Frank, Claudia Weber, and David Wood. "The Abuse of Animals and Domestic Violence: A National Survey of Shelters for Women Who Are Battered." *Society and Animals* 5.3 (1997): 205–18. Print.

Atwood, Roger. "Peru's Mummy Dogs." *Archeology* 60.1 (2007). Web. May 6, 2013.

Balter, Michael. "Dogs Gone Mad." *ScienceNOW*. 2006. Web. May 6, 2013.

Beyond the Myth: A Film about Pit Bulls and Breed Discrimination. Dir. Libby Sherill. Cover Ya'll Productions, 2010. DVD.

Bolton, Sarah Knowles. *Our Devoted Friend the Dog*. Boston: L. C. Page, 1901. Print.

Bartram, David J., and D. S. Baldwin. "Veterinary Surgeons and Suicides: A Structured Review of Possible Influences on Increased Risk." *Veterinary Record* 166.13 (2010): 388–97. Print.

Brandes, Stanley. "The Meaning of American Pet Cemetery Gravestones." *Ethnology* 48.2 (2009): 99–118. Academic Search Complete. Web. May 3, 2013.

Brantley, Alan C. "An FBI Perspective on Animal Cruelty." Interview by Randall Lockwood and Ann W. Church. *The Link between Animal Abuse and Human Violence*. Ed. Andrew Linzey. Brighton, UK: Sussex Academic Press, 2009. 223–27. Print.

Bustad, Leo, and Linda Hines. "Relief and Prevention of Grief." *Pet Loss and Human Bereavement*. Ed. William Kay et al. Ames: Iowa State University Press, 1986. 70–81. Print.

"Costly Monuments in This Cemetery for Favorite Dogs of Wealthy New Yorkers." *Syracuse Herald* July 6, 1919. Print.

Cowles, Kathleen. "The Death of a Pet: Human Responses to the Breaking of the Bond." *Pets and the Family*. Ed. Marvin B. Sussman. New York: Haworth Press, 1985. 135–48. Print.

DeGioia, Phyllis, and Edie Lau. "Veterinarians Prone to Suicide: Fact or Fiction?" *VIN News Service* (2011): n.p. Print.

"Dogs That Changed the World: Selective Breeding Problems." *Nature*. PBS. 2007. TV.

"Dorothy Harrison Eustis (1886–1946): A Biographical Sketch." *Journal of Special Education* 15.4 (1981): 410–11. Print.

Doty, Mark. *Dog Years*. New York: HarperCollins, 2007. Print.

Drysdale, John. *Our Peaceable Kingdom: The Photographs of John Drysdale*. New York: St. Martin's Press, 2000. Print.

Eau Claire County Humane Association. "Animal Statistics 2012–2009." 2012. Web. May 20, 2013.

———. "Cost of Pet Ownership." 2014. Web. July 1, 2013.

Eau Claire Police Department. Incident Report. August 9, 2013. Print.

———. Voluntary Witness Statements. July 23–24, 2013. Print.

Eustis, Dorothy. "The Seeing Eye." *Saturday Evening Post* November 5, 1927. Print.

Flaim, Denise. "People Who Believe in Afterlife Want One for Pets." *Chicago Tribune* January 10, 2007. Print.

Friedmann, E., and H. Son. "The Human–Companion Animal Bond: How Humans Benefit." *Veterinary Clinics of North America Small Animal Practice* 39.5 (2009): 291–326. Print.

———. "Who Picture." Pet-Abuse.com. Web. June 30, 2013.

———. "Why Do People Abuse Animals?" Pet-Abuse.com. Web. June 30, 2013.

Gates of Heaven. Dir. Errol Morris. IFC Films, 1978. DVD.

Grier, Katherine C. *Pets in America: A History*. New York: Harcourt, 2006. Print.

Humane Society of the United States. "Animal Cruelty Facts and Statistics." July 21, 2011. Web. June 30, 2013.

———. "Pet Overpopulation." Web. August 9, 2014.

———. "Puppy Mills: Facts and Figures." Web. September 17, 2013.

Kellert, Stephen R., and Alan R. Felthous. "Childhood Cruelty toward Animals among Criminals and Non-criminals." *Human Relations* 38 (1985): 1113–29. Print.

King, Barbara J. *How Animals Grieve*. Chicago: University of Chicago Press, 2013. Print.

Knight, Sarah, and Victoria Edwards. "In the Company of Wolves: The Physical, Social, and Psychological Benefits of Dog Ownership." *Journal of Aging and Health* 20.4 (2008): 437–55. Print.

Levinson, Boris. "Grief at the Loss of a Pet." *Pet Loss and Human Bereavement*. Ed. William Kay et al. Ames: Iowa State University Press, 1986. 51–64. Print.

Luke, Carter, Arnold Arluke, and Jack Levin. *Cruelty to Animals and Other Crimes*. Massachusetts Society for the Prevention of Cruelty to Animals and Northeastern University, 1997. Print.

Maddie's Fund. "Finding Homes for Senior Pets." 2007. Web. July 1, 2013.

———. "Marvelously Mature." September 2011. Web. July 1, 2013.

———. "Muttville Nation: A Community in Love with Senior Dogs." September 2012. Web. July 1, 2013.

———. "Sherri Franklin: Fairy Godmother to Senior Dog." June 2010. Web. July 1, 2013.

Maeterlinck, Maurice. *Our Friend the Dog*. New York: Dodd, Mead, 1905. Print.

Martin, Edward C., Jr. *Dr. Johnson's Apple Orchard: The Story of American's First Pet Cemetery*. Paducah KY: Hartsdale Canine Cemetery, 1997. Print.

———. *The Peaceable Kingdom in Hartsdale: America's First Pet Cemetery*. Lulu.com, 2010. Print.

McConnell, Patricia. *The Other End of the Leash*. New York: Ballantine Books, 2002. Print.

Miller, Geoffrey David. "Attitudes toward Dogs in Ancient Israel: A Reassessment." *Journal for the Study of the Old Testament* 32.4 (2008): 487–500. Print.

Moussaieff Masson, Jeffrey. *Dogs Never Lie about Love*. New York: Crown, 1997. Print.

"Mummified Dogs: Best Friends Forever." *Maclean's* 119.41 (2006): 31. Academic Search Complete. Web. May 3, 2013.

Muttville Senior Dog Rescue. "Awards and Accomplishments." Web. August 9, 2014.

Nazario, Brunilda. "27 Ways Pets Can Improve Your Health." WebMD. July 20, 2012. Web. August 9, 2014.

"NC Shelter Kills 99% of Animals, Records Show." WRAL.com. November 15, 2012. Web. July 2013.

O'Brien, Christena. "Chippewa Valley Experts Help Animals with Disabilities and Injuries Move Forward with Life." *Eau Claire Leader-Telegram* May 5, 2013. Print.

O'Rourke, Morgan. "High Suicide Risk for British Veterinarians." *Risk Management Monitor* March 29, 2010, n.p. Print.

Ostermeier, Mark. "History of Guide Dog Use by Veterans." *Military Medicine* 175.8 (2010): 587–93. Print.

Parham, Gregory. "Remarks by Administrator Dr. Gregory Parham, APHIS Public Meeting for Stakeholders." *APHIS Remarks* (U.S. Department of Agriculture, Animal and Plant Health Inspection Service) February 27, 2012. Print.

People for the Ethical Treatment of Animals (PETA). "Puppy Mills." Web. July 2013.

Petfinder. "Should You Adopt a Puppy or an Adult or Senior Dog?" *Adopted Dog Bible*. Web. July 1, 2013.

"Photo in the News: Dog Mummies Found in Ancient Peru Pet Cemetery."
National Geographic September 26, 2006. Web. January 2013.

Platt, Belinda, et al. "Suicidality in the Veterinary Profession." *Crisis* 33.5 (2012):
280–89. Print.

Recruiter.com. "Salary for Animal Control Workers." 2014. Web. September
2014.

Richards, Brent, et al. "Gonadectomy Negatively Impacts Social Behavior of
Adolescent Male Primates." *Hormones and Behavior* 56.1 (2009): 140–
48. Print.

Robinson, Lawrence, and Jeanne Segal. "The Therapeutic and Health Benefits
of Pets." Helpguide.org. Web. January 2014.

Santos, Fernanda. "A Rescued Goat Gets a Chance for a Normal Life." *New
York Times* May 1, 2008. Print.

Sayre, Carolyn. "The Wild World of Animal Prostheses." *Time* August 23, 2007.
Print.

Schneider, Katherine. *To the Left of Inspiration: Adventures in Living with Disabilities.* Indianapolis: Dog Ear Publishing, 2005. Print.

Seeing Eye, The. "Frequently Asked Questions." 2013. Web. June 1, 2013.

———. "Mission, Vision and Goals." 2013. Web. June 1, 2013.

———."Our Mission & History." 2013. Web. June 1, 2013.

Senior Dog Project. "Top Ten Reasons to Adopt an Older Dog." Web. July
1, 2013.

Siebert, Charles. "The Animal-Cruelty Syndrome." *New York Times* June 11,
2010. Print.

Skloot, Rebecca. "Creature Comforts." *New York Times* December 31, 2008.
Print.

Stager, Lawrence. "Why Were Hundreds of Dogs Buried at Ashkelon?" *Bar
Magazine* June 2010. Web. May 6, 2013.

Thurston, Mary. *The Lost History of the Canine Race.* Kansas City: Andrews
and McMeel, 1996. Print.

———. National Register for Historic Places application. Print.

"Top Dogs in Pet Cemeteries," *USA Today* October 13, 2000. Print.

"2012 United States Federal Budget." *Wikipedia.* May 28, 2013. Web. July 1, 2013.

United Cerebral Palsy of Philadelphia and Vicinity. "The Benefits of Pet Therapy." January 2, 2014. Web. August 9, 2014.

Wapnish, Paula, and Brian Hesse. "Pampered Pooches or Plain Pariahs? The
Ashkelon Dog Burials." *Biblical Archeologist* 56.2 (1993). Web. May 6, 2013.

Watkins, Tom. "Paper Delves into British Veterinarians' High Suicide Risk."
CNN.com. March 26, 2010. Web. June 30, 2013.

Weeks, Linton. "The Recession and Pets: Hard Times for Snoopy." *All Things Considered*. National Public Radio. April 6, 2009. Radio.

"Where New York's 'Smart Dogs' Find Last Resting Place." *New York Times* September 3, 1905. Print.

Whitaker, Barbara. "Building a Stairway to Paradise, for Your Beloved Pet." *New York Times* January 14, 2007. Print.

Whitcomb, Rachel. "Understanding Pet Overpopulation." *DVM: The Newsmagazine of Veterinary Medicine* April 2010: 30, 32. Web. July 1, 2013.

"Wills of Some Prove Unusual." *Daily Messenger* December 1, 1932. Print.

Worden, Amy. "More U.S. Pet Owners Turn to Pet Insurance to Protect Four-Legged Friends." Philly.com. January 4, 2012. Web. July 2013.

Wormerly, Katherine. *Our Domestic Animals: Their Habits, Intelligence, and Usefulness*. Boston: Ginn, 1907. Print.

You, Jenny. "Two Dogs Attack Pet Cat, Dangerous Dog Law Could Be Reviewed." WEAU.com. August 1, 2013. Web. August 10, 2013.